VOLUME 3

WAITING IN THE

PIT

STORIES OF BROKENNESS, BENEVOLENCE, BLESSINGS AND BREAKTHROUGHS

VISIONARY AUTHOR

HILETTE A. VIRGO

Unless otherwise stated, all Scripture quotations are from the Holy Bible, King James Version KJV (Authorized version). First published in 1611. Quoted from the KJV Classic Reference Bible, Copyright 1983, by the Zondervan Corporation.

DEDICATION

To the soul who is in life's pit stop being fueled and serviced by the Creator.

---- 66 ----

"The Lord is good to those who wait for him, to the soul who seeks him."
(Lamentations 3:25)

---- 99 ----

CONTENTS

INTRODUCTION

The Pit Stop

"Hilette, I don't know God's plans for you or how this is all going to play out, but it is evident that God is stretching you."

I was in Virginia, conversing with Uncle Rocky on the phone, detailing the trials and tribulations I had endured since I left Georgia for New York. I had found myself on the cusp of homelessness in New York and was miraculously delivered by a friend turned sister who invited me and my two children to drive seven and a half hours in the middle of winter to Virginia to stay with her and her four children in her three-bedroom house. I was expressing for the umpteenth time how frustrated I was about my journey and my exhaustion in waiting for God to deliver and give me a breakthrough.

"Hilette, I have no doubt God is with you and is using you," he continued. "We just have to wait and see how this is all going to pan out."

Wait. I groaned inwardly. Oh, I had grown to loathe that word. How much longer, God? Why do I seem to always be in the throes of waiting?

This was a few weeks before I had a divine encounter, during which God commissioned me to start the *Waiting in the Pit* series: a collection of three books over a three-year span. The series, as the name suggests, is about the transformative power of waiting amid life's challenges, and it was this concept that God had chosen me to explore and share with others.

A year and a half later, I had returned to the state of Georgia and settled in a three-bedroom basement apartment with my two children in the home of one of the elders for a church that had finally become home. Like many times before, Brother Gray commended my ministry and encouraged me to be steadfast.

"Hilette, after this is all done, you will be an expert on the matter of waiting. You will have a degree in it and will be giving talks all over on the subject of *waiting*. People will be intrigued and find you credible because of all your experiences."

That word again!

I had completed two volumes of the three, following the timeline God had given, and was experiencing a different level of testing at that juncture. I couldn't wait to complete volume three. I couldn't wait to free myself from the burden of responsibility and anticipation accompanying the mission. Still, more than anything else, I couldn't wait to receive the breakthrough God had promised.

Later that evening, I mused on what Elder Gray had said. I don't think he understood the magnitude of his words. Three years to write three books, collaborating with over fifty saints representing over twenty countries from diverse backgrounds, all under one mission. Why me? Why did God choose me to spearhead this mission? How could He trust the person who consistently declared with great confidence and without an ounce or semblance of remorse for years, "Patience is a virtue I do not possess." What was the purpose of it all?

Over the three years from 2022 to 2024 of working on this project, I experienced diverse levels of emotions, numerous stages of frustration, and infinite volumes of apprehension. As expressed by one author in volume two, I felt like I was in a coal pit, layered and stacked tightly and being pressed under intense compression. I could also feel the penetrating heat in the fire of my trials. I also felt like I was being pruned and pried open for some sort of surgery.

I watched a video where a guy was encouraging people to plant fruits, and, in some instances, he advised them to cut open the seed pit to remove the embryo to sprout it. Many times, I could feel God's knife removing my hard outer layer and cutting me open so He could work on my heart. Then, there were days I felt spiritually lifeless, and I could tell that He had me nestled in the giant pit of His hand as He allowed me to rest or was performing CPR on me.

There were days I felt like I was indeed undertaking an undergraduate study and was failing my courses and had to constantly repeat modules and retake exams. And as expressed in the introduction of volume 2, there were moments I resented God and felt He was asking too much of me. There were days I felt like He abandoned me and was carrying me on a meaningless ride. Yes, I saw what He was doing for others, but a sermon preached by my pastor's wife resonated and kept echoing in my mind, "What about me, Lord?"

Many of the co-authors shared their healing journey and the breakthroughs they experienced in their relationships. They all agreed that participating in this project had shifted their mindset and accelerated their ministry. Their stories were inspiring, and I was genuinely happy for them. But amidst their success, I couldn't help but wonder, "Lord, what about me?"

I was flush in the middle of turmoil after witnessing yet again breakthroughs from authors who participated in volume two when I remembered the promise God gave me after complaining bitterly post volume one, "Your breakthrough is at the end of volume 3, Hilette."

Following this memory, I felt like I had been injected with a fresh dose of hope. A *breakthrough was* on the horizon, and I was ready for it. God had promised *it*, and I was certain He would deliver *just* as I had envisioned.

The new year began, and I was determined to complete this third volume. Candice and Seri, who had experienced God's blessings and personal growth through their contributions in the first two volumes, were equally committed. They expressed their interest in completing the 'waiting course' and contributing to the third volume, standing in solidarity with me.

Maria, having been thoroughly blessed by volume one as a reader and then in volume two as a writer, and having discovered and sharpened her hosting skills during the subsequent "Pit Stop" (an online weekly podcast-style event where all the authors were interviewed), decided that she, too, would not be left behind and would also share in the third volume.

I felt relieved and blessed. All three ladies committed to writing in this volume and formed a team to hold up my aching arms, as did Aaron and Hur in Exodus 17:12 during the Battle of Rephidim against the Amalekites. Was I in a battle? I surely was—an intense one at that. In the same manner that Moses realized that the Israelites were winning while his hands were raised in prayer and losing when his hands sagged in exhaustion, I encountered the same pressures during this process. Thanks to the "dream team," which led me to sit on the Rock of Ages and stood beside and behind me in the middle of the battle, I completed this volume through tears, agony, and immense frustration.

But let's talk about the six months "pit stop" leading up to the release.

The journey started with immense ease. Maria and Candice managed the administrative processes intricately. Under the leadership of the Holy Spirit, they identified and selected the 21 team members to complete this final volume. The energy was high, and the pit crew was briefed on their roles and responsibilities.

As we held our first sets of "meet and greets" and "writers training," I shifted into cruise gear. For the 1st time in three years, I did not have to do everything singlehandedly. *I see You, God; You are making this one very easy for me. You know how exhausted I have been, and You know I need all the assistance and support for this last leg.* Everything was falling into place. The crew was aware of the deadlines, and everyone felt confident about their roles. I sang high praises and expressed my appreciation for the executive team, comprising the three ladies, and the crew's resilience and determination to get the "Royal Ride" to the finish line in grand style. Seri had started the cover design, and we all agreed that purple was perfect for the grand finale.

I was beaming! I now had less responsibility since I had the team working alongside me. There was nothing much to do until the chapters were submitted. As the authors toiled on their chapters, I decided to test-drive the "Royal Ride." I have always liked long road trips and didn't mind doing it solo. I had taken fourteen-hour trips with my children, going through multiple states, all while processing my thoughts and daydreaming as they slept most of the way. Hence, here I was, waiting for the authors to complete their assignments while musing and daydreaming about my breakthrough. Yes, the one God *owed me*. I envisioned how it all would come through.

When I started volume one, I envisioned that by volume three, I would be married and writing about it. I envisioned my husband writing a chapter as well. That was now Candice's story. I was a little disappointed that it would not be likely that I would have a dramatic love story to share in four months, but maybe God would start writing my love story within this short time so I could hint at it by the time I started writing the introduction.

I started obsessing and daydreaming about the way God would deliver my heart's desires. Of course, he was going to give me *this*. He definitely would be coming through with *that*. Things would finally fall into place. I was excited to see Him deliver others on the journey. I had witnessed Him pulling authors out of their financial pits, landing them new jobs, mending their broken relationships, delivering husbands, elevating their ministry, and many others. I knew what I needed. I knew the pits I was in. Of course, God knew them, too, and would surely pull me out from every single one of them!

"Delight thyself also in the Lord: and he shall give thee the desires of thine heart. Commit thy way unto the Lord; trust also in him; and he shall bring it to pass" (Psalm 37:4).

I know I was a complainer sometimes, but wasn't I delighting in Him? Wasn't this project evidence of me committing my way to Him? What about my other ministries? Indeed, God would not lie. I heard Him clearly. He told me my breakthrough was at the end of this project.

As I watched the days take flight and as the hours and minutes ticked on toward the finishing line, I started encountering every mechanical challenge possible. I started losing power in my spiritual engine. The more I mused, the bumpier the ride got. If God was going to come through on one specific desire, shouldn't I be seeing the evidence already? I didn't feel as confident as before. I started doubting the idea of breakthroughs. My faith took a nosedive into a ditch, in which I had broken my mental headlights and scratched and twisted my emotional bumper.

Additionally, the wheels of my car were no longer aligned, and I started feeling unworthy. This was followed by bouts of confusion, and the "what ifs" started gushing from leaks in my engine's heat and power steering hoses. What if I had imagined all of this? What if I had canceled or aborted God's plan for me through disobedience and unbelief? What if I was unworthy? What if this was all a figment of my imagination and this was not a God mission?

I was losing control and felt like I was hydroplaning in murky waters.

After sputtering over a short distance, I realized I had no choice but to make a spiritual "Pit Stop." I had to coast the vehicle into a divine rest and servicing area and submit my heart, mind, and spirit to celestial servicing and refueling. After taking inventory and assessing the damage to my soul's engine and shell, the diagnosis was that I was running on incorrect fuel. I was not following the driver's manual (the Bible) or allowing the angelic mechanical host and the Holy Spirit to service me daily. For a long time, I lost sight and understanding of the purpose and value of the mission God had given me. For three years, I had held on to the notion that God had a particular obligation to provide me with the things I had listed and was waiting on because I was working for His cause, and He was coming through for others, so He had to come through for me. Was this all fueled by the desire for personal gain? Was I doing this for selfish reasons?

My engine flatlined.

I realized I was imposing a timeline on God and setting myself up for possible disappointment and discouragement. What if the things I was demanding of God weren't what He had in mind for me? Who knows God's thoughts? Only the Spirit of God knows God's thoughts.

"For what man knoweth the things of a man, save the spirit of man which is in him? Even so the things of God knoweth no man, but the Spirit of God." (1 Corinthians 2:11)

Was I only serving and trusting God for what He could do for me? Would I love Him still even if He had not come through for me? Was my faith contingent on God's rescuing and relieving or Him delivering my desirables? I thought of the Waldensians who followed God in poverty and simplicity. They had given up everything for the cause of Christ. They were willing to die in His service, expecting no earthly reward. I thought of the great martyrs during the Dark Ages, who had given their lives for God as they fixed their eyes on heavenly attainment. What have I truly done for God? Did I see Him as an ATM where I would use Him for financial and material gains? Was I holding God up at gunpoint, demanding Him to fulfill my earthly and carnal desires and not genuinely desiring Him? Then, what if the breakthrough was more spiritual than physical? Wouldn't that be a far more noble and advantageous cause?

As the crew started submitting their chapters, I realized how vain some of my requests were. While contemplating the various themes and testimonies shared in all three volumes and seeing where many of the authors were and what some had lost and were experiencing, I started adjusting my thoughts. I was blessed in more ways than I cared to admit. I had taken this journey and missed many of the scenic views because I was trapped in my thoughts and expectations on the ride.

God *owed me* nothing. He did not owe me a breakthrough. He had no obligation to give me exactly what I *wanted*, and in His infinite wisdom, He had no need to come through exactly how I anticipated. Like a helpless child, I had a track record of desiring things that were not good for me. Too many times, God had to show me the dangers I craved and how He saved me by not giving me what I wanted. He impressed on my heart: "You didn't get what you wanted; you got better."

Indeed, God had me on a course and was constantly recalibrating my mental engine. He was adjusting its control parameters to optimize my spiritual walk. For the significant part of three years, I was obsessed with gaining specific breakthroughs, but I missed the revolutions I had received along the way. He had strengthened my spiritual muscles and enlarged my territory. God had given me the beautiful honor of spearheading a team of multitalented and multifaceted individuals across the globe. He had used me to help many birth books and ministries. He had given me a front-row seat to witness His children grow and glow in Him.

As I replayed the events leading up to the release of this third volume, I saw how God had elevated and sustained me. I started the journey almost homeless, and He rescued and established me and gave me a supportive and loving church family. I keep telling my friends how I have grown over the last year. There were many things I demanded, but I had matured enough to realize I was not ready and still may not be ready to receive.

I thought about Elizabeth and Zachariah (John the Baptist's parents), who desired a child but did not receive one after years of waiting. They had passed the years of childbearing and were evidently contented because the Bible described them as righteous. "And they were both righteous before God, walking in all the commandments and ordinances of the Lord blameless" (Luke 1:6). They had trusted God even when He did not come through for them. Zachariah still performed his priestly rites, and Elizabeth maintained her sweet demeanor. They were both now "stricken in years" and had released their parental dream. Yet, God came through for them after they had waited and evidently shelved the thought. Can we still love and trust God even when He doesn't come through for us?

Our stories will not be the same. The woman with the issue of blood waited 12 years to be healed, the woman bent over waited 18 years to be straightened, Joseph waited 22 years for the fulfillment of his dream, David waited 15 years after his anointing to become King, Jesus waited 33 years to start his earthly ministry officially, Jacob waited 7 years for Rachel and 14 years to be freed from Laban, Noah waited 120 years to see God fulfill the prophecy of the flood. Abraham and all the patriarchs had to wait on God for short, medium, and long term desires. Many got what they wanted, others didn't, yet they still trusted God.

After three years, I realized I was in great company. All God's children must wait at some point in their walk with Him. Waiting is a high and noble calling, and it strengthens our trust and dependence on God. It also facilitates our growth, development, and maturity in Christ. It is excruciating but extremely necessary to wait on God. We are all in the "Pit Stop" of life, being fueled and serviced by God for a higher calling. I thank Him for calling and choosing me for this great mission. I release my obsession for a tangible breakthrough. I had almost missed the spiritual revolution and acknowledged the breakthroughs I was receiving along the way because earthly pleasures and treasures blinded me.

I have learned not to lay up treasures on earth that are susceptible to destruction but to invest in heavenly bonds. (Matthew 16:19-21)

Over the past three years, God has brought me through an intense course of unlearning, learning, and relearning. In year one, He brought me back to the basics. He had my mother share the story of my birth and how she had waited on God for me in the first volume. Additionally, He connected me with the people I needed at that time and had them share their stories to bolster me on the journey. In year two, He revealed how He was waiting on me when I thought I was waiting on Him, and now He has shown me the value and blessing in the wait.

Significantly, I realize that God owes me nothing! I owe Him everything. As the author in Lamentation expressed:

"My strength and my hope are perished from the Lord: Remembering mine affliction and my misery, the wormwood and the gall. My soul hath them still in remembrance and is humbled in me. This I recall to my mind, therefore have I hope. It is of the Lord's mercies that we are not consumed, because his compassions fail not. They are new every morning: great is thy faithfulness. The Lord is my portion, saith my soul; therefore will I hope in him. **The Lord is good unto them that wait for him, to the soul that seeketh him. It is good that a man should both hope and quietly wait for the salvation of the Lord."** Lamentations 3:18-26)

I no longer demand God come through for me on my terms. Whatever His will, I am content to trust Him and know that His ways and His plans are perfect.

I pray that as you read the foregoing stories of brokenness, blessings, benevolence, and breakthroughs, your soul will be stirred, and you will come to appreciate the working of God in your life. Whether you are in a dug-out pit, a fruit pit, a coal pit, the pit of God's hand, an orchestra pit, a pilot pit, or whatever pit you are in, know that we are all in the same "pit stop" waiting as we are being serviced, fueled and prepared for the second coming of Christ. I pray you will wait well and trust God to direct, realign, recalibrate, restore, reward, revitalize, renew, and keep you steadfast.

Meet the Visionary Author

Hilette A. Virgo is a brand plucked from the fire. A woman striving after God's heart, she is a Christian life coach, international preacher, poet, songwriter, transformational speaker, bestselling author, publisher, editor, ghostwriter, and book coach.

Hilette is on a mission to uplift, inspire, and empower people to "Tap into their GREATNEST and Soar into their GREATNESS" through her calling of writing, speaking, and coaching.

She firmly believes that every soul that has graced this earth with their presence possesses a wealth of inexhaustible potential waiting to be harnessed, including you. She also believes everyone has a story and a testimony that will be the rope of hope to pull a stranded soul from their pit and help another to cope. She is the visionary author of the Waiting in the Pit series and has authored, ghost-written, edited, and published hundreds of books.

Known to her clients as "Mommy Eagle" and "The Book Doula," Hilette is determined to convince everyone she meets of their inner GREATNESS, one written and spoken word at a time!

ACKNOWLEDGEMENT

Special thanks to the twenty-one mechanical workers (the pit crew), each with their unique skills and expertise, who said yes to helping to furnish the "Royal Ride" for this literary expedition. Your individual contributions have been invaluable, and we are grateful for your dedication and service.

Your meticulous work in aligning the tires, cleaning the windshield, calibrating the engine, and all the other tasks, has been instrumental in preparing this ride to bless others. Your role is crucial, and we are deeply appreciative of your efforts.

Our heartfelt thanks go to Miguel Lowe, whose meticulous care in removing the scratches and dents and polishing the ride to perfection truly made it royal. Miguel, we deeply appreciate your efforts.

Special thanks to our executive and technical managers, Serena Rowe, Candice Andrews-Bailey and Maria Urassa. Thanks, Serena and Colbert for the beautiful cover designs, trailers, and mockups to promote this production and thanks

Maria and Candice for your arduous and selfless service in managing the mechanical staff.

The Lord has done it once more, and we are grateful. Blessed be His name.

CHAPTER 1

What if I Told You that God Restores?

"

For I will restore health unto thee, and I will heal thee of thy wounds, saith the LORD; because they called thee an Outcast, saying, this is Zion, whom no man seeks after.
(Jeremiah 30:17)

"

I had just finished crying my eyes out in the passenger seat of my husband's white Tesla car. Her name is Leesa, and I felt comfortable crying in the cuddle of a chrome-tanned leather upholstery for the first time in my life. It wasn't anything he said that triggered the floodgates of water mixed with salt from the 6-ounce servings of Wendy's French fries we had grabbed on our way or the fact that I just came from a health class and felt guilty eating junk food, and it wasn't that PMS never seems to leave me alone. It was simply my engine overheating. I was burnt out and tired from going all day.

For a second, my spinning world stopped. I had to depress my mental brakes, and as soon as the pedal hit the floor of my frontal lobe, a heaviness of overwhelm covered me like a thick dark cloud. I couldn't understand it. I am in a happy marriage, and the ministry is going great. Why do I feel empty? God has given me what I asked for, and now I'm crying like a four-year-old who had her iPad taken away by her parents. If I'm honest with myself, it's because when God massively restores you, as He did me, you feel you owe the world and God your all. Yet, you can't give both God and the world all of you; it's only one you get to choose. In one breath, I felt like I needed to heal the world, and I couldn't even sing like MJ to start. On the other hand, I wanted to be the best wife, church member, employee, friend, sister, and family member all day. I wanted to make it evident that I was healed and happy.

Under all the parading, I was still hurting and not coming to terms with the culture shock, the new environment, and having to adjust to life in a country where you need a credit card to do almost everything. I hate sounding like I am ranting and complaining, but I must tell you the truth. God restores, but restoration is not a destination. It is a journey with twists and turns and numerous pit stops along the way, and we must stick it out with Him so He can show us how to manage the emotions, energy, and thoughts we experience when He restores us.

When the tires of my life got flat, my windscreen smashed, my airbags deployed, and when my engine light turned red, God never stopped being my Mechanical Engineer. As you read this chapter, I hope you have had the opportunity or will get a chance to tour volumes 1 and 2 in the *Waiting in the Pit* series. Though they glorified God, those stories were seasoned with tears and sighs, and I begged myself not to write another sad story so the world could know that the God I serve is restored. Hence, come along with me on this ride as I tell you how God took me from a crumbled junk and made me into a sleek, state-of-the-art spiritual machinery for Him.

I feel like I got an electronic upgrade, and like Nick's car, I am more innovative and efficient. Was it as easy as swiping your loaded credited card at a dealership? No! The restorative process came with growing pains, countless highs and lows, and was a process that could not be rushed or cheated. I had to grow through it. I had to be crushed and recycled. The Mechanical Engineer had to remodel and reconfigure me. I am still in the process of being programmed, and I am always conscious of it. It would make all of heaven and my pit crew sad if I didn't tell you how God restored and rescued me after I had crashed and crumbled.

Writing is a healing activity for me, and I never know where to start, but I place my fingers on the keyboard by faith and hope that God will guide the words and make them flow. To understand this restoration story, I must take you back to the day I got that text. It was an invitation to write. Ever since I can remember, I have wanted to be a writer. The feelings were mixed because I didn't see myself as a great grammar-ready girl. Even though I spoke well enough, my writing was never my strong suit. You would think that I would be confident in writing for someone who owns more books than clothes, but I have major insecurities when it comes to expressing myself on paper or screen. Yet, my writing is my safe space, and I feel free when these words get out.

So, about that text message. It was an invitation to become a co-author in the book *Waiting in the Pit*. I remember the face of the visionary author. I had a super huge crush on her work and how she showed up, and I wanted to be a part of her space. This was one step closer to the possibility of being an author. I took the bait and said yes. The writing journey started for me, and there was no turning back. In volume one, I wrote about grappling with grief and dealing with my father's death. I was nine years old when I experienced my first crash. My life was written off when my father died. Many things died with him, and I didn't understand how to handle grief. I struggled for years, scooting in and out of the hospital, lived an on-the-edge life, and tried to keep sober about my future. After 22 years of carrying the pain of his death in the trunk of my mind, God allowed the *Waiting in the Pit Volume 1* book to become the moment of freedom for me.

My freedom journey was real. For the first time in years, I felt lifted; my mindset was different, and I felt the weight of carrying the grief floating away with every word I wrote. It was the first time I witnessed my pain processed on paper. I would have written plays and poetry in the past, but something about this prose process was different. It was like a deliverance service, a baptism, a purification by fire, like driving on a clear highway. I was free. Free knowing that my father is asleep in the grave. Free knowing that he isn't in heaven, looking down on me with pity. I'm free, knowing he wouldn't haunt me in my sleep because I never got to say goodbye to him. I am set free, knowing that even though my earthly father died, my heavenly Father is still alive and well.

The chapter was entitled "Something Has to Die for Something to Live." I didn't understand why that title came to me, but it felt right. The old me had to die so I could finally live the life God had in store for me. My mindset about life and death, emotions, desires, and chemical makeup needed a reset. Writing that chapter helped me support myself and others in finding coping mechanisms to heal and grow from grief.

However, before the book could move from being published to print, I received the worst possible news a young, trying woman could ever hear. The man I was seriously involved with and preparing to marry died from a sudden heart attack. My world suddenly froze. The same feeling of instant emptiness that I felt when my father died came crashing into me at 100 mph. My engine felt like it was knocked from my shell. Sharing this now makes my stomach cramp, but I need to get it out so this story can get the justice it deserves.

The next few months were rough. I had just come off my social media soapbox, stating that I was healed from the grief I had carried for 22 years. Now, after climbing the rope out of one pit, I slid down the slope of grief into another pit. My life looked like a game of snakes and ladders, except there were no snakes, and I needed a ladder. Life had just taken another twist, a detour. The grief was intense but felt different this time around. It was a whirlwind. Not again! This experience made me feel cursed and confused. Why would God make me meet this man? Why did He allow me to fall in love, make life plans, and then take him? It didn't make sense.

Nothing makes sense when you serve God yet seem to be going through a series of unfortunate events. Yet something in me was still fighting. There was a flicker of light in me to keep going; my battery still had some spark. In that low and dark moment, I was nudged on my shoulder by my guardian angel to return to my safe space of writing. In the middle of counseling one evening, I heard my engine humming. God was starting something yet again in me. *Candice, just write about it.* So, I got on the phone with my editor from the pit crew and told her, "Hey, I have a book in me." My mind started to swirl with ideas, titles, and themes for the book. I lived in a colorful past, so the book was already completed in my mind before one word landed on the page. Pushing through the pain, I was able to birth a whole book. One year after losing, I received a box from Amazon with 50 copies of my first book, *The Stretched-Out Life*: *Trusting the Process of Being Pulled, Pressed, and Pushed by God*.

This book came when I needed to process every significant issue in my life and release it. I may sound biased here, but I put a lot of sweat into that book. I pushed and pressed so hard to complete and birth it. It helped me in a dark time, and those who have read it said they were blessed and had no clue that that was my life under the plastered smile I wore daily.

The opportunity to write knocked on my door a third time. This time, it was to contribute to book 2 of the series *Waiting in the Pit*. Volume 2 came when I was ready to process more of my life on the pages. I was prepared to address the deep pit of depression that seemed to revisit me now that I was single and alone. I remember the process as if it was just yesterday. The chapter title for volume 2 was "Why Live When You Want to Die?" God was showing me a pattern here. Life is like a racetrack, and God always keeps His Pit Stop open 24/7 for our restoration. My engine needed to be serviced, and He wanted to process me for the journey He had prepared for me. I felt like God was releasing me from the cloud of the grief pit to deal with the deep press of the depression pit.

Dealing with depression was excruciating for me. Most times, I tried to hide it, and other times, I aired it out for all to witness. I was angry, hurt, ashamed, rejected, and empty once again. My love tank was low, and I felt like I had written a thesis paper for a master's in clinical psychology with this chapter on depression. God gave me space to accommodate, and I was impressed to swallow my pride and return to the singles ministry. I never thought that in 1000 years, I would be walking back through the virtual doors of the singles ministry. This could not be happening. It all felt like I was starting over. Who would want me? I had mileage on me; men might see me as a used car since the world knew that that "yardie" man I was with had died. No one would want me in their showroom.

I was wounded, bruised, beaten, and bitter. I kept hearing the words "Serve." Serve? After I was dealt a lousy hand of cards after I was embarrassed and depressed? Whatever happened to the saying, "You can't pour from an empty cup?" I was empty, and God felt distant. Counseling took its course, and I agreed with all of heaven that I would return to ministry and join the single souls waiting in the lobby to be taken by someone. Little did I know that heaven was up to something, and the pit crew had a massive surprise for me.

After six months back and fully serving in ministry, one night hosting an event changed my life forever. A message popped up on my Zoom dashboard at the height of my presentation. Why? I wasn't ready to open to meet another racer, and I didn't want to break my focus on the track. It was a faceless male interested in communicating with me. I gave him my number out of respect and left right after my presentation. I left that Zoom room and returned to my waterbed of tears because I was not married and didn't get my happily ever after. Healing came, and so did a message from the unknown male. What started as me playing hard to get turned into a long-distance love story. The messages never stopped flowing, the calls never stopped coming, and my heart felt light again.

Love flowed in my tank from a premium pump. This racer jumpstarted my engine, making my world happier and my heart healthier. Wait, the best part is the text led to calls, the calls led to visits, and the visits turned into me making a move that changed my life. 2023 saw my life picking up speed when the unknown male became my boyfriend and partner in pre-engagement counseling sessions. Things grew rapidly, our wheels were spinning, and before I knew it, he was meeting my family, I was meeting his, and our love grew wings.

Some months passed, and my life took on a new meaning. I am running out of gas and words to tell you all the details. Just know that God restored me full circle, and I am so grateful to God for the comfort He brought into my life. The comfort felt like the comfort of the leather seat I sat in earlier tonight. Before I could make sense of the string of blessings flowing my way, I moved from girlfriend to fiancé to a whole wife. How did it happen? Ask God! I am still in awe.

It went like this: I sought help, started serving, opened up, trusted God, took the risk, and now I'm here. I am no longer Candice Marie Andrews but now Candice Marie Bailey. I, Mrs. Bailey, need to share what restored means to me. This is what restoration looks like:

R – Repositioning happens when God is getting ready to repair you. Everything happened so fast. Before I knew it, I was off the land and in the air, heading to meet up with Mr. Bailey, not knowing that he would ask me to be his wife in a few months. Things took flight literally. When God is getting ready to restore you, He doesn't leave you in the same place. The blessing in store will be found in a new space and environment, nothing like what you are used to.

In this season, you must trust Him and the process He is bringing you through. Today, I was repositioned—migrated, married, and in ministry with my husband, Nicholas. Don't be afraid. Sometimes, God must shift you to bless you. I call this step the alignment phase. If your alignment is bad, your journey will be shaky, and you will be veering off course or even crashing. God wants to reposition and re-align and order your life.

E: Equipped to endure. When God restores, He doesn't only reposition you; He equips you for the move. He gives you everything you would need for the journey, and there are some things He allows you to collect along the way. When He calls you to move, He will also equip you to endure and to stand. God allowed me to write to heal and equipped me with a coping technique. At this stage, God gives you spare tires, a car jack, jumper cables, and products to freshen and clean your vehicle seats.

S: Supply is in the storehouse of heaven. Every need He will supply. That's what restoration looks like—supplying your needs and replenishing your losses. When you are with God, you can never lose, and you will never be lost. When heaven is your storehouse, you never run out of oil, coolant, and windshield wash. The Spirit of God gives you oil to keep you on this powerful journey, keeps your mind calm, and helps you maintain a clear vision.

T: Therapy helps process the pain. Counseling and doing the work to be healed is part of the restorative process. Restoration is on the other side of processing the pain. Therapy is a vital healing step. Therapy is like having an earthly mechanic giving you frequent management checks. In restoration, God must become your spiritual Mechanic. You must trust Him to take care of and heal you.

O: The opportunity to testify. When God restores, He allows you to tell your story so that He can get the glory. It's also an opportunity to turn your pain into a product. The byproducts became the book and a ministry. When God restores you, He expects you to stop your vehicle and take the opportunity to carry others around in your car. You can't stop for anyone and everyone, but you won't drive into heaven alone. Your healing is an opportunity to help other passengers along the way.

R: Recharge your spirit. I have learned that when God restores, He recharges your spirit to renew and revive you to serve Him better. At this stage, God has elevated you and is charging you faster than a Tesla supercharger station. We must be recharged, so stand still and allow God to fill us up.

E: Encourage others to trust God's process. When God restores you instantly, you become a spiritual statistic of the goodness of God. At this stage, God tests us to see if we will pull our cars over when we see others in the emergency lane with a flat tire. We can't drive by in our fancy cars and drive past those who need help in the shoulder lane.

As I write, in a few weeks, I will be five months happily married. I am living not only "the stretched-out life" but the restored life. Restoration feels so good. When I was in my pit of depression and grief, marriage left like a distant dream for me. Now, gratitude is all I know. The overwhelming feeling I felt earlier is lifted because I remember God is still writing my story. The crying in the car was a release to start writing this chapter. Sitting at my desk, I am reminded that God keeps His promises. In December 2022, God said He would restore it all. I had no clue it would look like this. When God restores, He gives you more than you deserve and heals you ten times better than before you were hurt.

It's 12:07am, 2/22/2024. I am at peace knowing that I serve a God who is invested in my happiness, and He is also invested in yours. I want to end my chapter by saying the pit was never meant to be a permanent place; it's just a processing plant. He refines us in the pit and leaves us sparkling new to carry on the next leg of the journey.

I wish you could have seen the happiness on my face at my wedding. It was the glow of a girl who became a woman and was grateful that God didn't give up on her. Whoever you are and wherever you are, it's not over. God has the final say. Trust Him as the Mechanic who will restore your life's vehicle, and you will never live a day of regret. Back home in

Trinidad, when we get a new car, we ask spiritual leaders to bless it. I invite you to pray over your life and let God take the wheel. Nothing was more healing than hearing my husband's words as he sat beside me, planning the wedding. He said, "Candice put these words on the program for our wedding."

"Intreat me not to leave thee,

Or to return from following after thee:

"For whither thou go, I will go, and where Thou lodgest, I will lodge: Thy people shall be my people, And thy God, my God." Ruth 1:16

In my heart, I felt peace come over me, followed by a dose of doubt. What if I fall? What if I fail? Then I looked at him and thought, *what if I soar, and what if I told you that God shall restore?*

He restored my soul; he leads me in the paths of righteousness for His name's sake (Psalm 23:3). I am safe, I am loved, I am free. God restored me.

Meet Candice Andrews-Bailey

Candice is a devoted daughter of God and servant of the King of Kings, blessed to be married to Nicholas Bailey. An author, educator, and mental health advocate, she has a passion for supporting individuals dealing with grief, depression, and anxiety. Her book, The Stretched-Out Life, explores the process of being pressed, pulled, and pushed by God.

Originally a secondary school theatre arts teacher in Trinidad, Candice has since moved and founded a ministry for women aspiring to marriage while overcoming mental health challenges. She previously served as a radio host on Adventist Radio London. Candice firmly believes in Christ as our only hope for salvation and eagerly anticipates His second coming.

As the second of five children, she credits God for her gifts of authorship and speaking, which she uses to share biblical truths. Featured on various faith-based podcasts and Hope Channel's "Let's Pray," Candice continues to support women through coaching and mental health programs.

CHAPTER 2

"Can Somebody Help me please! JamJam's not Breathing!"

> ❝
>
> *Trust in the Lord with all thine heart; and lean not unto thine own understanding. In all thy ways acknowledge him, and he shall direct thy paths. (**Proverbs 3:5-6 KJV**)*
>
> ❞

I pressed the red panic button and sounded the alarm. I reached for the ambulatory bag (manual resuscitator) and turned the dial on the oxygen cylinder to its maximum output. "Come on, JamJam, breathe, breathe," I pleaded as I tickled his toes and feet, desperately trying to stimulate him. "Okay, JamJam, Mummy is going to tilt your head back slightly to open your airway, please baby, please breathe." I placed the mask over his mouth and nose, ensuring I had a good seal, and gently squeezed the bag to administer the first rescue breath and followed the protocol. Check; there are no breathing sounds, and no chest rise. Second squeeze, check; no breathing sounds, no chest rise. Third squeeze, check; no breathing sounds, no chest rise. "Come on, JamJam. Please, God, please!" I always called upon our Heavenly Father for help in those moments. Fourth squeeze, check; the grey color that had slowly overcome his face, languidly dissipated like breath against a mirror fading. The colors expressing signs of life crept back into his cheeks, freeing the dusky grey and blue tinges from their frightful presence.

My husband and our other children filled the room as they took on their well-rehearsed roles. My teenage son was on the phone with the paramedics, reading from the emergency card detailing JamJam's main conditions and highlighting that he had an ambulance directive. My middle daughter connected him to the oxygen saturation monitor, which, once hooked up, would reveal to us how much or, more realistically, how little oxygen was circulating through his body. My youngest daughter was praying, and our 5-year-old stood staring helplessly, taking it all in. This was nothing new; it was just another time that first responders and paramedics would fill our home with blue lights flashing outside our front door.

This regular occurrence was typically triggered by a seizure or central apnea. My husband, dashing between checking JamJam's prepacked hospital bag and making feeds to take with us, would quickly roll JamJam's rug and remove his soft blue play mats before the paramedics arrived. Many of them had visited our address before and knew us well.

"This is JamJam."

"I've been here before..."

"NO! Not there! Mum doesn't like us putting anything on his bed."

Jermiah-Lee, also known as JamJam, was born with a rare chromosome disorder that affects approximately 2 in every 10,000 children in the UK. In short, an extra copy of chromosome 13 is produced, and instead of the usual pair of chromosomes, three copies of the thirteenth chromosome are present in the cells. There are varying presentations of Patau Syndrome Full Trisomy 13 (FT13), formally called Patau Syndrome, where an extra copy of the thirteenth chromosome presents itself in every body cell. It is the most extreme form of the condition. JamJam was born with Full Trisomy 13 (FT13).

I was 16 weeks pregnant when doctors confirmed the diagnosis on August 16th, 2017. "I am so sorry; the test results are positive for Trisomy 13," expressed the geneticist on the other end of the telephone. My heart sank into a pit of despair and brokenness. My husband and I just held each other as frightful thoughts flooded our minds, accompanied by silent screams and unspoken pain. Somesthesis engulfed my body as the thud of my heart, the enveloping arms of my husband, and every gut action became heightened and deafening in the silence of the still room. We were eventually released from our helpless embrace. I went into the bathroom and wept bitterly, calling upon my heavenly Father to wrap His arms of love and protection around our unborn child. Our geneticist explained that we could terminate the pregnancy at any point.

A decision needed to be made quickly. I was given two options.

Option 1: Before twenty-two weeks, I would be given tablets to end the pregnancy; two days later, I would be hospitalized to start the process of induced labor and give birth.

Option 2: After twenty-two weeks, a needle would be placed into my abdomen, injecting a fluid directly through my baby boy's chest and into his beating heart to end his life.

In both scenarios, I would deliver a dead baby. We rejected both options. Our final decision was to trust God and allow our unborn child to write his story.

My daily tears of anguish became tears of vivacity and passion once we overcame the turmoil of indecision and

WAITING IN THE PIT

finally agreed that we wanted our son to have a chance at life. I determined at that moment that I would rely fervently upon the leading of our heavenly Father.

"Trust in the Lord with all thine heart; and lean not unto thine own understanding. In all thy ways acknowledge him, and he shall direct thy paths," (Proverbs 3:5-6 KJV) *was* the scripture that governed my thoughts and actions going forward. It's a scripture that has taken me through many of life's tribulations and one that I needed more than ever in this journey.

Our JamJam, as I often refer to him, was born via cesarean section on Wednesday, January 10th, 2018. He was born not breathing and required immediate medical intervention. I remember eventually hearing his feeble squeal once the doctors managed to get him breathing. It was the most beautiful and reassuring sound. He'd made it through the first hurdle.

JamJam was born without eyes, but God miraculously gave him eyes at eight months, a testimony for another book. He was diagnosed as blind, but God gave him visual perception. JamJam was diagnosed as deaf shortly after birth, but God miraculously gave him hearing. He was born with polydactyl of the limbs, six fingers, and six toes on each hand and foot. He had heart and kidney issues alongside many other complications, including central apnoea, meaning he would have pauses in his breathing and, therefore, stop breathing.

He also had medication-resistant epilepsy, was non-verbal, and was fully tube-fed.

JamJam loved music. At the sound of any beat, his eyes would widen, his head would start moving, and his entire body would enjoy the rhythm. He especially loved the sound of the guitar; happiness filled his soul during his weekly music therapy sessions.

My life was committed to caring for JamJam. Every moment was dedicated to loving and giving my utmost to meet his needs. I poured my love into JamJam like an everlasting, ever-flowing well. I was meticulous with him. I gave him the absolute best of myself, and he deserved it. Nothing was too big or too small for me to do for him.

I relied upon the leading and guidance of our Heavenly Father for everything with JamJam. I would pray for wisdom over every decision I made about his care. "Lord, should I move him this way." "Lord, should I give him this medication." "Lord, should we take him to the zoo or the park?" "Lord, please guide me as I care for your son." I knew nothing could be achieved in my strength, so I relied entirely upon God.

We spent many days, weeks, and even months in hospital throughout JamJam's life. We were often told, "JamJam is dying." I rebuked those words, sometimes audibly but often in my heart each time. I was convinced that despite his life-limiting condition and prognosis, whenever that time came for my son to breathe his final breath, God would prepare me. Until then, I was disinterested in any negativity.

On June 19th, 2022, on Father's Day, JamJam was admitted into the hospital. He had picked up a virus, and this had triggered multiple seizures and apnoeic episodes. He spent 7-months in intensive care and 3-months in the main ward. Every day was a battle. I was bound by a chasm of anguish, desperate for my son to get through the illness. Navigating family life was tough, but navigating the medical system was even more overbearing. Weekly meetings with consultants from various teams, including palliative care, were taxing and emotionally draining, but we never gave up hope. It was always our plan to bring our beautiful boy back home. When faced with a situation where you have two conflicting and opposing parallels, your mind can become overwhelmed with confusion; the medical world tells you about their medical viewpoint versus the power of God.

On October 11th, 2022, my family was informed that JamJam had hours to live. We were placed in a private room in the intensive care ward and told to call our loved ones. My husband and I sat in a meeting room, and the process was explained to us. They informed us about our choices and what would happen to the body. They took us through the process of determining the death and what checks would be made.

A dear sister of mine entered the room that day. It was filled with the morose sense of despair and helplessness from all present. Her bright smile beamed across the room, and she prayed and sang hymns and praises to God over JamJam. JamJam took his rattle beside him and slowly moved it to the rhythm of the hymn. Within hours, he was moved out of the private room and returned to the ward. I knew it was not his time. God had not given me that conviction. JamJam was still fighting.

After nine months in the hospital, JamJam was discharged on a palliative pathway. He received a standing ovation from the staff at the hospital as we walked towards the lift through the row of staff lined up on either side of us. It was a surreal and beautiful experience to bring JamJam back home where he belonged. He was on a ventilator for 24 hours a day and was still very poorly. Throughout his hospital admissions, he had overcome so much. He had made significant progress, and at times, things looked positive.

My family and I were determined for JamJam to live the most colorful and beautiful life for as long as we were blessed to have him. With the support of our palliative care team, between Wednesday, the 20th to Friday the 23rd March, 2022, JamJam was granted a once-in-a-lifetime wish through the phenomenal charity Make a Wish UK. Our family enjoyed an all-expenses paid trip to Centre Parcs in Woburn. The planning was intensive. JamJam's presentation substantiated our palliative care team's concerns. He had significantly changed; the medical team would use the word "declined." But we held on to hope in God's restorative power.

We packed with an abundance of medical equipment and supplies, including symptom management medications and the dreaded end-of-life medications. Throughout our journey and visit to Centre Parcs, JamJam's vital statistics were the best since returning home. He physiologically showed us that he was happy and enjoyed being connected to nature and taking in the natural sunlight and freshness of the crisp morning air. The concerns that JamJam may die on the journey to or from Centre Parcs or while we were there were overshadowed by the improvement, we witnessed in him. I had every faith that it was the right decision because a friend of mine had committed to praying and fasting on our behalf, and God had given us, through her prayers, obvious signs to go ahead. We moved in pure, unadulterated faith. We created and cataloged the most beautiful experiences together. Collaboratively, we had given JamJam a transcendent experience with his family, led by God, that is incised within my heart forever.

James 5:15-17 (NKJV): "And the prayer of faith will save the sick, and the Lord will raise him up. And if he has committed sins, he will be forgiven..."

I would read this scripture, clinging to every word, claiming it as I prayed over JamJam. I had every faith that God would save my son. There was nothing within me that doubted.

On the morning of March 29th, 2023, four weeks after returning home, JamJam had a significant desaturation at approximately 5:30 am. His night nurse had pressed the emergency button; JamJam wasn't breathing. I tried my utmost to revive him. It took all that I had to keep him going. We praised God that he started breathing again but had to administer 15 litres of oxygen through his ventilator.

JamJam had the most incredible home nurses. They were a super team and worked collaboratively to ensure he received the best possible care. His day nurse, Stef, was one whom we trusted, and she knew him exceptionally well. I was confident he would be in good hands and that I didn't need to stay with her throughout the shift as she was very competent. When she arrived, I did our usual handover detailing the events of earlier that morning. We washed JamJam together. I prayed over him from the crown of his head to the soles of his feet, which had become my usual morning routine. I'd lay my hands on each part of his body and petitioned the healing power of God over every internal organ. I informed Stef that I would get on with some cleaning and would be available if she needed me. I immersed myself in cleaning, and as I mopped the kitchen floor, the Holy Spirit prompted me to STOP cleaning and GO spend time with JamJam.

At approximately 11.30 am, JamJam had another significant apnoea, which mirrored the earlier one. Stef and I struggled to get him to breathe again. The ambulatory bag was again proving to be inefficient, so I gave rescue breaths using mouth-to-mouth resuscitation. We managed to get him to breathe once again. I knew that things were different and that something wasn't quite right. I lay in the bed beside my son, and I held him. We played all the songs he loved: "Jireh" by Elevation Worship, "The Goodness of God," Bethel music, and many more.

At 1:30 pm, JamJam had another significant desaturation. His oxygen saturation on the monitor plummeted even more profoundly than the previous two. Stef fought with all her might to "bag him" and get him breathing again. For me, the intervention was just too much, and I told her to stop and put him back on the ventilator. We called our palliative care team and told them what was happening. The response at the end of the phone was, "I think JamJam is trying to tell us something." I rolled my eyes and prayed in my heart. I wondered if this was another occasion where they would tell us JamJam was dying, and he would again prove them wrong. I was advised to call my husband, Darren, after which I called my mum and closest friends.

When my husband arrived, I was sitting on the nursing chair with JamJam in my lap, lying across my arms. Darren sat beside me, and suddenly, my vision became unclear due to a mist in front of me. I rubbed my eyes, closed them, and opened them again; the mist was still there. I asked Darren if the diffuser was on, and he replied, "No." I asked him where the mist came from, and his response was, "What mist?" It was as clear as the back of my hand, right there in front of me, undeniable and visible in plain sight. I knew at that moment that was my sign. God was preparing me for the worst moment of my life. I felt as though an angelic being was present to usher my son into the hands of God. I prayed and asked God to show me what to do and guide me in supporting JamJam best. In the most painful and excruciating moment of my life, I was able to keep calm and rest assured in Jesus.

JamJam's siblings, our closest family members, friends, and home nurses filled the room. There was an atmosphere of peaceful lament, ambient yet sorrowful. Together, we sang to JamJam, read his book, *JamJam Can!*, and talked to him, letting him know we will all be reunited one day, and the next face he would see is that of our Lord and Saviour, Jesus Christ. I told him that his body would be perfected, and we would all be reunited as we enter the kingdom of heaven. I reassured him that he didn't need to be afraid, that mummy was with him. I also spoke to JamJam about his new PeaPod chair, which was due to arrive in the next two weeks. I told him he should fight and get through this moment if he wanted to enjoy that chair. However, if he was tired and wanted to rest, Mummy would accept that, and he had my permission to do so. Shortly after, JamJam gave a final gasp. He took his last breath and died in my arms, surrounded by his siblings, closest family members, friends, and nurses. I screamed in indescribable agony and cried out to God.

JamJam had remained calm throughout; his nurses who were present described his death as the most beautiful and peaceful they'd ever witnessed. My love for JamJam was a love I will never experience again. I love all my children with all my heart and soul. But the love I had for JamJam was different. He relied upon me for his every need. He could not do anything at all for himself. Absolutely nothing. I was his advocate. JamJam was an incredibly gorgeous boy, with skin fair and golden like rich honey and brown curly hair that felt like silk as it slipped through my fingers. His hair would often have streaks of blond and gold in the summer, and when he smiled, you just had to smile, too. I seriously took my role and commission to God as JamJam's mum. I was proud to be chosen and handpicked by God to care for this precious child. The connection I had with my son was deep-rooted and beautiful. Strong, symbolic, and woven together like the roots of the most magnificent redwood tree. God saved JamJam, not in the way I had desired, but God saved him from his earthly tribulation and gave him the gift of eternal life.

The scripture in Romans 5:1-5 holds significance to me; it describes the journey I am on. At the time of writing, it has been almost a year since our JamJam died. I struggle in my grief. The pain of losing my beautiful boy is unbearable and gnaws away at me daily. It often consumes and engulfs me. Moreover, I glorify God in this tribulation because I know this death is not final. Through my adversity, I have learned what it means to persevere. My character is being refined daily. I live in the hope of being reunited with JamJam. I have become more forgiving, patient, and less consumed by the things of this world. Nothing on earth is worth forsaking the opportunity to live for eternity with my Lord and Savior, united with my precious boy. My hope in Jesus propels me forward each day; it gives me a purpose to hold onto.

I often tell myself that I would rather live my life as if there is a God and die to find out there isn't, rather than live as if there isn't and die to find out that there is. This way, I have nothing to lose. The value and peace I receive through my faith isn't comparable to anything. In my most challenging moments, I can turn my eyes toward Jesus and know I have hope for a better world. He counts every teardrop and understands our pain. He died as a living sacrifice to save us from our sins; through His spilled blood, we are redeemed.

I hope and pray that you will be encouraged by my sharing this intimate part of my life. I pray that if you don't already have faith in God, through this testimony, you will begin to experience and see the power of Jesus and make the decision today to give the God who saves, the God who loves you with an everlasting love, the opportunity to stand with you and lead you through your trials and tribulations.

Many people supported our family throughout JamJam's life. My heart desires that they will experience a personal relationship with our Heavenly Father so that on that great day, when this world as we know it comes to an end, they too will be reunited with our Savior. Jamjam can run into their arms, look into their eyes, and thank them for all they had done for him throughout his life on earth.

I look forward to that day when we live together in perfect harmony, death will no longer hold its power, pain will cease to exist, and eternal life with our Saviour and those we've loved and lost will be our reward.

I want to see you there.

Meet Serena Pascall

Serena Pascall is a devoted wife, mother, and woman of faith. She is passionate about sharing her journey with God.

She founded TriLife Education, where she raises awareness about disabilities through workshops. Serena authored JamJam Can!*, a children's picture book celebrating the wonderful tapestry of being different and born with complex needs.*

Serena is incredibly passionate about supporting families with disabled children. She is an early years family practitioner. Serena has shared her son JamJam's story on various media channels, including her blog, www.mumoffaith.com, podcasts, radio stations, magazines, and newspapers. Serena desires all to experience the beauty of a relationship with Jesus Christ. You can contact her at:

www.mumoffaith.com, www.TriLifeEducation.uk, Instagram: @mum.of.faith, Instagram: @JamJam.can, YouTube: @SerenaPascall9234

CHAPTER 3

Until the Altar

> **❝**
>
> *When the time is right, I, the Lord, will make it happen.* **(Isaiah 60:22)**
>
> **❞**

I was 23 years old when I decided that I'd abstain from sex until my wedding night. This was in line with my Christian beliefs, and as a young woman who was brought up in the church, I'd always been aware of God's expectations when it came to intimacy, which is that we should abstain until under the covenant of marriage.

Preserving one's purity and saving yourself for your future spouse is also highly commended in my Zimbabwean culture. However, prior to coming to the decision of abstinence, I was very much open to being intimate with a man before the altar, despite the explicit instruction from the word of God to do otherwise.

My thought process was that *if the man I loved and I went down the intimacy path, surely, in the eyes of the Most High God, the presence of the passion shared between my partner and I sufficed and equaled a marital covenant.* I was sure that God would wink at my disobedience and view it from a different light, even if my lover and I hadn't gone through the process of committing to each other and exchanging those eternally binding vows at the altar. To right the wrong, my long-term plan was to marry whomever I'd given myself to at some point in the future.

Various factors influenced my thinking, and among these factors was that, by the time I reached my late teens, most of my peers had either traded off their virginities or were on the verge of it. These peers included Christians and non-Christians alike and were quite open to sharing their experiences with me. I would sit and listen to the mythical tales of their first times—tales of passion, mingled breaths, and love declarations.

I remember one of my peers blissfully telling me that after spending her first night with her lover, he had professed to her that she was his and that she now belonged to him. For someone who'd always sought belonging, I felt as though I was missing out. I also concluded that their experiences sounded way too magical to have been wrong, let alone sinful.

While I waited to meet the one I'd finally belong to, I resorted to living vicariously through my friend's stories, praying, and wishing that someday, I, too, would be cherished and desired in such a way. To further my knowledge of intimacy, I took an interest in erotic and romantic literature. I spent much time daydreaming and fantasizing about my future lover and all the love and passion we would share.

Around that time, I was also writing short stories and poetry, and to liven up my writing, I started adding some mild, intimate scenes with enough detail to entice the imagination but not too much to cause alarm to those with whom I shared my writing. Somewhere along the way, it dawned on me that, unlike myself, the authors of most of the literature I was immersing myself in were writing from experience. This unnerved me, as I felt that I led a mundane life. What reader would be interested in reading the works of one who hadn't fully lived according to what I believed at the time?

Another factor was that I had the misfortune of falling for a young man who mocked me for still having been a virgin. This affected me in such a way that I shifted from merely wanting to be with someone so I could finally belong to despising and loathing my virginity and inexperience.

I would have given myself to the first man who made an advance on me to "liberate" myself and, finally, graduate from girlhood to "womanhood" as the world perceived it. However, something always held me back. Even then, my deepest desire was to experience and share the special moment with someone who would cherish me, and one I felt was worthy of me. So, despite my openness, somehow, I still wanted the security and sacredness found within the confines of a marital covenant. I'm convinced now that God is the one that placed that parameter within me, the one that had me refuse to go with just any man and less than what I deserved.

My frustration with the wait for "the special one" grew. I'd pray to God, asking him to send me someone I truly loved so I'd finally experience what my peers were experiencing. I grew impatient with God and battled with him nightly. Little did I know that He was protecting me from myself and all the consequences that often come with engaging in sex before marriage.

I remained open to premarital intimacy until the fateful age of 23 when I came across a young man whom I will call "Melvyn." I met him at an educational institution, and it took a lot of pursuing on his part before I would consider a friendship with him. When I finally let my guard down, I agreed to collaborate with him on several projects. I soon discovered that we both aspired for and shared the same dreams in the creative space, and we were romantically compatible. I would also learn that Melvyn was a driven young man with a clear vision for his future and a charismatic personality that matched his drive.

The more time we spent together, the more I started seeing some of the qualities that I'd always desired in a partner, and the more I started developing strong feelings for him. There was this all-consuming sense of euphoria and utter bliss in his presence. He would speak so highly of me, make me laugh, and challenge me in a way that forced me to see myself in a way I had never done before.

What I felt for him transcended mere physical attraction. It was the kind of feeling that burned through my soul and left me utterly speechless. Somehow, it was as though my and Melvyn's souls had been knitted together, as though we'd once upon a time been one, spiritually in another lifetime, as he very much felt like a familiar companion.

After a while of getting to know each other, he would confess his feelings for me, and when he did, I was filled with much joy. Melvyn would also go on to play a pivotal role at a very critical moment in my life, and somehow, through him, I was finally able to comprehend God's unconditional love for me and his faithfulness.

This man had been placed in my life at a time when I needed him the most, and he effortlessly fulfilled the role that he'd been cast to play ever so perfectly. I knew then that even if presented with the opportunity to be intimate with him, I would decline it without a second thought. How could I betray and dishonor the One who restored my faith in love and came through for me in my 11th hour? How?

"How then could I do such a wicked thing and sin against God?" **(Genesis 39:9)**

How had I convinced myself that dishonoring the Author of love and intimacy was acceptable? All in exchange for temporary pleasure. Oh, how foolish had I not comprehended that I'd only betray myself by disobeying God's command. **(1st Corinthians 6:18)**

My response to Melvyn's love profession shocked me, as I felt it necessary to share the decision that I had just made at that very moment, which was that I now intended to wait on God till marriage. The satisfaction from coming to this life-altering decision was replaced with disappointment and confusion. I soon found that while Melvyn admired and commended me for my conviction to honor God, he was on a different path. He explained that he still had a lot of areas that he needed to work on, which included his struggle with lust. This meant that we couldn't pursue anything romantic despite what we felt towards each other.

It suddenly dawned on me that I hadn't fully considered the implications of my decision and what that would entail for future relationships and lovers who had no desire to be celibate. Naturally, I was conflicted, for on the one hand, I had now chosen to align myself with God's will and principles, yet on the other, it meant losing this person with whom I had built a connection.

My first thought was why God presented me with Melvyn when He knew that he wasn't the one he had in mind for me. Why introduce us to each other and allow us to get close when we couldn't be together? It reminded me of when God asked Abraham to sacrifice Isaac, and it made me question why the Good Father would bestow one with their heart's uttermost desire and expect them to give it up.

At least in Abraham's case, God went on to present him with the sacrificial lamb so he wouldn't have to give up Isaac, his promise. I, on the other hand, spent months and nearly a year trying to come to terms with my short sojourn with Melvyn and all those memories that we had shared.

It wasn't until I healed that I understood the lessons God wanted me to take away from the experience. I would learn that, while nothing romantic had come out of my and Melvyn's encounter, I now knew the depths of what I was capable of feeling without having to physically involve myself with another being.

Because Melvyn chose to be transparent about the path that he was on, I didn't have to waste my time only to be disappointed in the long run. The Holy Spirit had led him to confess and reveal his lifestyle and convicted him to let me go. Thus, God spared me from potential heartbreak and soul ties that may have come if we'd pursued sexual relations.

God revealed to me that unlike Abraham, who went to the lengths of placing Isaac on the sacrificial altar, I wasn't ready to receive my promise, and I hadn't been prepared to put God first before my needs. I didn't trust Him enough to provide me with a similar or even more incredible blessing in the future.

I also feel that God wanted to teach me something about myself, about how He had created me, in such a way that I felt things deeply. This led me to understand that the intense feelings I'd felt for Melvyn should have only been reserved for my husband and explored in a space where I would feel safe and secure.

In Songs of Solomon 8:4, the women of Jerusalem are warned not to "stir up love, and to not awake it, until its ready." I had gone and stirred up love before its time before commitment, and it was only now that I understood why the women of Jerusalem were given that instruction. Even more importantly, I would realize that the decision to be abstinent was only the first step of the process. Like the journey of faith, it needed to be tried and proven before it passed the test. After coming to these realizations, I feel that's when my celibacy journey truly began.

WAITING IN THE PIT

The journey certainly hasn't been easy, and the tests have been countless. I have experienced my fair share of disappointments, doubt, and frustration in the waiting. I have encountered counterfeits, those who came masquerading in sheep's clothing, claiming that they were my answered prayer and those who have mocked me for choosing the path of purity.

I have laid down in the nights, weeping myself to sleep and questioning if I'm enough or if I'm making the right decision in keeping to my principles. Though I have tried my best, I have found myself in a similar space to the one I was in after Melvyn, where I have wondered why I must continue waiting on God when I have purposed in my heart to honor Him.

There have been occasions when I have sat in the waiting room of life, watching the invisible biological clock of my womanhood tick away. With each tick, my chances of marrying and conceiving the children that I so very much desire to bring into the world decreased.

I have also had moments where my faith was renewed, and I pondered on the miracle that Sarah experienced in her nineties, with the birth of Isaac, and how God kept His promise, in that she went on to be the mother of nations **(Genesis 17:16)**; of Hannah's answered prayer in Samuel, and the story of how Joseph, after his faithfulness to the Lord, went from the pit to the prison, and from the prison to the palace; how Christ, waited thirty years of his life, to finally start His ministry; David waited around 14 years post his anointing as king to reign as one, and how Joshua waited for the promised land.

I have scrolled through the archives of my mind, gazing through the history of God's faithfulness in my life, the breakthroughs and answered prayers, and how He made beauty out of the ashes of my life. So, despite the challenges, setbacks, and moments of doubt, I have come to the resolve to trust and praise Him while I tarry here. For I, too, like Sarah, choose to "believe Him" as I have "judged Him faithful who has promised" **(Hebrews 11:11).**

Somewhere along the way, I have been inspired to be a better "waiter," to wait expectantly and patiently. I have come to embrace and love my name – PATIENCE. "Knowing this, that the testing of your faith, worketh, PATIENCE" (James 1:3). I'm beginning to live out my name, to find beauty in it all. Slowly but surely, I'm getting there.

Yet, more importantly, I have shifted my mindset from viewing my future husband as the reward for waiting to see Christ as my prize! He is, after all, the ultimate bridegroom and my first love. I'm also viewing celibacy and waiting on God as a blessing. In celibacy, I am covered and veiled until the time is right.

And while I wait, I continue to lift my eyes to the hills, from whenceforth cometh my help, and in faith, I'm transported to my wedding day, to the one from whose rib I was taken. In faith, I'm all made up and attired in my wedding gown, a veil covers my face, and the "Here Comes the Bride" instrumental plays in the background. Family and friends stand to their feet, cheering me on.

In faith, I behold the one my Father ordained for me from the very foundations of the earth. I exhale and smile just before taking the first step down the aisle. Then, I begin to glide, headed for the altar. And the closer I get to my groom, I cannot help but praise my Heavenly Father. I can't help but be in awe of his faithfulness.

And I'm singing Naomi Raine's song *(The Story I'll Tell)* in my head:

And I'll testify of the battles You've won

How You were my portion when there wasn't enough

And I'll testify of the seas that we've crossed

The waters You parted, the waves that I've walked.

Singing, oh-oh-oh, my God did not fail (Yeah)

Oh-oh-oh, it's the story I'll tell

Singing, oh-oh-oh, I know it is well

Oh-oh-oh, it's the story I'll tell

My Father kept His promise! My God did not fail; He can't ever fail! He was preserving me for a purpose, and the wait was worth it!

Within moments, I'm transported back to the present, and I'm smiling still and praising Him for all that's to come. I'm "calling those things that are not, as though they were" (Romans 4:17), and I'm confident in doing this because I'm "judging him faithful who has promised" (Hebrews 11:11). I'm basking in the wait and "laughing at days to come" (Proverbs 31:25), and it's all because of the joy my Father has set before me (Hebrews 12:2).

And look at all this beauty He has allowed me to behold in faith!

So, until I encounter the one, I can confidently declare that "I have found the one whom my soul loveth" (Songs of Solomon 3:4), not only because of all the emotions I'll experience but also because of the commitment and covenant we will make before God and my loved ones. I will choose to be patient.

Until I receive the go-ahead from my Heavenly Father, I will continue to trust Him who is unfailing.

Till I find the one who exhibits the characteristics required of a godly husband in (Ephesians 5:25-33), I will wait, even *until the altar*. For waiting on God is of the highest and most significant of honor. Thus, my conviction has also led me to renew the vow that I made to God all those many years ago. And to mark this renewal, I have decided to start a celibacy ministry.

The ministry *encourages women to abstain from premarital sex and refrain from all sexual activities until they are married. This is in accordance with the biblical principle, which instructs Christians to maintain sexual purity and save it for the confines of a marital covenant. It welcomes women of all ages, backgrounds, and cultures to join the celibacy path. A journey that promises no material rewards or gain but one where we see Christ as the prize! Our gratification comes from knowing that our Father will be most pleased with us for choosing to honor Him in such a way until the altar & beyond.*

Trusting and believing that: "When the time is right, the Lord will make it happen" (Isaiah 60:22)

Meet Patience Chitiyo

Patience Chitiyo is a creative production coordinator, assistant theatre director, aspiring producer, and poet with a passion for storytelling. As a production coordinator, she coordinated and oversaw logistics for CNN Create's local and international short-form documentaries and branded content campaigns.

She holds a BA in Experimental Film Making and a master's in producing for television and film. Hailing from the vibrant landscapes of Zimbabwe, Patience spent her formative years steeped in culture and community. Now based in the United Kingdom, she brings a global perspective to her work. Beyond her professional pursuits, Patience is a dedicated advocate for godly womanhood and social justice.

Driven by her conviction to honor her Heavenly Father and His instruction around premarital sex, Patience is on a mission to launch "Until the Altar," a ministry that encourages women to maintain their purity and remain celibate till they are married.

CHAPTER 4

Divine Detours: Navigating God's Blessings in Unexpected Places

———— **❝** ————

And we know that all things work together for good to them that love God, to them who are the called according to his purpose. ***(Romans 8:28 KJV)***

———— **❞** ————

In 2014, I officially migrated to the United States of America despite my prior dislike for the country. I was never inclined to visit for vacation or live in the US, but God had other plans.

A few years before moving, I was diagnosed with uterine fibroids, which were growing at a rapid rate and required surgery. I took my vacation and traveled to the USA on my brother's invitation for a two-week vacation, which turned into a month and then years.

During my vacation, I met a friend who later became my partner. He encouraged me to have the surgery done in the USA, citing that it would be better for my recovery. I agreed and made the necessary arrangements for the surgery, hence my extended stay.

Little did I know that God, in His divine providence, was preparing the way for me through unorthodox means. I entered the USA using my visitor's visa and was given six months to stay, which was the norm. However, I only had two weeks off from work. During my stay, I encountered some severe pains in my abdomen. I initially thought it was just gas pains, but they turned out to be pains caused by the fibroids resting on my uterus. My brother and his family advised me to visit the hospital, and I was admitted to facilitate further tests and told that I needed to have the surgery done immediately. I was now in a dilemma. My health was at stake, but doing the surgery meant taking more time from work. I had exhausted all my vacation and leave time, so I either had to take the risk of losing my job or forfeiting the surgery and risking my health. I was at a dicey crossroads because, besides my sustenance, I was responsible for paying my parent's mortgage. I needed God's direction desperately because I was confused.

The time drew closer for me to return to work, and I had an appointment at the hospital in New York to undergo surgery two weeks after my return date. What was I supposed to do? My anxiety increased as I contemplated the decision. On the day designated for my departure, I decided to return home; hence, the surgery was not done, and the problem with my health persisted. I didn't know it then, but God was setting things up for me.

I spent a few months at home, and as I mentioned, my friend encouraged me to return to get the surgery done. I left my beautiful island country home yet again to do the surgery in the "land of opportunities" with plans to return after recovery. I visited the hospital and had to go through the testing period all over again. I was told that generally, once you've been given a surgery date and didn't show, it was difficult or impossible to secure a new appointment. But God is a God who makes the impossible possible. I got a date and completed the surgery successfully.

I spent about a week in the hospital and was then discharged with instructions to return for outpatient care. On my first visit to the nurse, I experienced pain like no other. After examining the wound, she observed that I had internal drainage. This could have caused infection if it was not dealt with urgently. She informed me that she would have to reopen the wound and clean it, which she did. I felt the most excruciating pain I have ever experienced in my life because she did the procedure without giving me an anesthetic. In that moment, I was reminded of the pain Jesus suffered for me and the pruning process we go through to become more like Him.

Because the wound was reopened, I was instructed to visit the hospital every day until the wound was healed. I had already exhausted my vacation days, so I had to apply for sick leave. I only had a week's worth of sick days, which was not enough time for recovery as I was in no shape to return to work. So, what was I to do? I prayed but like many other times, the answer never came how and when I expected it. I decided to rest and go along with the moment because we never know what God is planning.

I was incapacitated and had to depend on others. My friend, who by then became my partner, took on the responsibility of caring for me. I needed more time after the week I was given because I was not yet cleared for work. I applied for extra time, and though it was granted initially, I was later sent a dismissal letter. To my dismay and chagrin, I lost my job as an assistant financial officer with the airport company in Saint Vincent and the Grenadines. I was infuriated, anxious, scared, perplexed, and worried. How would I provide for my parents or pay the mortgage for my home?

I only had a visitor's visa, which meant I could not work in the USA legally; I would have to return to my country and seek other employment. I couldn't see my way out, and no quick solution came to mind. Throughout my recovery, I prayed God would work things out. By then, I had moved in and was living with my partner. We were not married, and I knew this was not right in the sight of God. I felt I couldn't do better, but this was because I was not depending on God to fix the situation; I was trying to fix it myself. Yet, in His mercies, God miraculously solved my problem. I was introduced to the idea of acquiring an internship visa, which would allow me to work legally with a company in the USA.

Months passed, and I finally recovered to my optimal health. I was healthy and strong but jobless. I had no idea how I would subsist financially, but I trusted God. With the help of my partner, I began the application process for the internship visa (J1). Surprisingly, it took a shorter period than expected. While the visa was being approved, I had to return to my home country. I knew having the visa didn't guarantee a job, and even if I got one, it would be for 18 months, which was equivalent to the visa's timeframe. Yet, in my desperation to find employment, I ignored all the uneasiness I was experiencing in my spirit. I was returning to a strange country to seek employment while entangled and ensnared in an ungodly relationship.

In my mind, I was constantly reminded that I was living contrary to God's plan, yet I felt hopeless to do anything about it. Let me inject here that the enemy makes our wrongs seem justified in our eyes, and he sugarcoats our situations to blind us from the truth. I was promised marriage in this relationship, and though he was much older than I was, had mature college-aged children, and was separated (not divorced or single), I pushed all the warning signals aside and pushed on, hoping it worked out while ignoring the Holy Spirit's chastening.

That relationship lasted for a few years, but like anything not founded on Christ, it soon crumbled. Unfortunately, I didn't escape unscathed. I still bear the scars as reminders that only God can orchestrate a life that works together for His good. This relationship damaged my self-esteem to the point of powerlessness. Many people experience abuse in diverse ways and levels; mine came through verbal and psychological abuse. This trampled my self-worth and confidence. On many occasions, I was reprimanded for wanting to do more or progress in my life. There was subtle manipulation, and he always wanted to maintain control. I was picked up and dropped off everywhere I needed to go. I was prohibited from attending business meetings because he thought I was cheating on him. As time progressed, my self-value diminished to zero.

We both attended church, yet I felt that the word of God wasn't taking root in my life because I was returning to the same life Sunday after Sunday. My self-esteem deteriorated to the point where all I did was go to work and then return home to drown myself in Netflix shows to avoid addressing the situation. I felt constantly bombarded by depressive thoughts. I became ashamed to even look at myself in the mirror. *Who am I? and What have I become?* I asked myself over and over. *What am I doing living with someone who isn't my husband?* Questions popped constantly in my mind, slathered with myriad insecurities.

I grew up in a Christian home and had the vision of getting married and living a wholesome Christian life, yet here I was, caught in a relationship that was not fulfilling the purpose God had for me. I was not content with living contrary to God's will. However, I felt trapped and helpless to escape because of financial constraints. My lack of trust in God to provide kept me shackled. Then, one day, I was scrolling through the TV channels, and God planted a seed in my mind through a minister who said: "You are God's big idea; stop living small and selling yourself short." I immediately felt the tug in my heart shift, and this began my journey out of the pit of a spiritually and emotionally toxic relationship. I consecrated more time to God, read His words, and filled my spirit with praise, knowing He would work things out. My transformation didn't happen automatically or overnight, but God did it.

I was now working with a prominent non-profit organization, and the time came for my visa renewal. I was instructed to leave the country while my new visa was processed. I still believe this was God's way of breaking the spell of entanglement off me. I left the country intending to have the visa renewed and return to work within 3-5 days. Instead, the process took three months. I felt distressed, but God was working in mysterious ways. He wanted me in an environment where He could work more on my heart uninterrupted. He positioned me where I had to confront and deal with my situation. I was in a season of reflection. God took me back to my roots, allowing me to worship at my childhood church and reconnect with Him. I recognized how much I needed God and decided to trust Him to see me through.

My visa finally came through, and I returned to the US with the intention of changing my living arrangement and living fully for Christ. However, with all good intentions, those plans went through the window when I examined my situation. I had nowhere else to go and no one else to turn to. Confronted with this renewed desire to serve God in the right way and the desperate situation before me, I chose the easy way out. I continued living with my partner.

I am certain that God does not leave His children until He has gotten them where He needs them. He pursued me relentlessly in my pit. As the relationship continued, it gradually deteriorated and with it went my self-worth. I tried to counsel myself that the relationship was temporary, yet I found no consolation in that thought. I knew I wanted to get out but didn't know how to. I fought consistently with the Holy Spirit, who assured me I was a masterpiece. How could that be true when this was my lot? His constant beckoning ignited a burning desire for change and growth in my mind, yet the thought of being homeless kept me bound. Still, God, in His infinite mercy, didn't leave me alone. He divinely orchestrated my escape plan through a stranger who later was engrafted into my family.

I had started a network marketing business that occupied my time and mind so I did not become depressed. One day, I was invited by my co-worker to attend a tea party and create a display table of products. I accepted her invitation and suggestion. Of the many persons who visited my table that night, God instructed me to call one person from the contact list I curated. I will call him Matthew. Through Matthew, who I later learned was a minister, God intensified His work in me. Matthew called me almost every day, and sometimes, for what seemed like hours, he spoke life into me.

When he learned of my situation, he ministered to me gently and compassionately, much like Jesus did with the woman of Samaria at the well. He built up my belief in the power of God to change and bolstered my confidence to embrace myself as a woman created by God for good works. I began to see the relationship I was in for what it was: a distraction from Satan to distort my destiny. I started to formulate a plan to extract myself from this lifeless relationship, and the desire grew stronger each day.

After this divine intervention, my partner and I started butting heads regularly. I was accused of cheating on him with Matthew (which was not the truth) and later found out that he was the one cheating with an old girlfriend of his who had just gotten married to another man. Though I knew I wanted to leave that unfavorable relationship, the pain of that revelation broke my heart to shards. I felt the sting of rejection and pain. It was an attack on my self-worth, self-esteem, and identity. I found myself succumbing to guilt and shame. I decided this was my lot because of my inconsistencies with God; He was punishing me for my infringements before Him. I cried incessantly. I felt disgusted, blamed myself for the situation, and even developed self-disdain. Yet God, in His great love, pursued me relentlessly.

I had ceased communicating with Matthew to prevent any further accusations, but God continued to use him to pull me out of the pit. God paved the way for my exit by allowing a room in my brother's apartment to become vacant. I immediately moved in and started my journey into healing and developing a deeper and more intimate relationship with God. Matthew introduced me to his cousin's church, where

God cushioned and nurtured me into the woman He originally planned for me to be. All things were indeed working for my good.

The journey after that proved challenging, and I wasn't quite prepared for it. I now had to cover all my financial expenses (which I didn't need to do before) while continuing to pay my parent's mortgage and contributing to their welfare. This was a major adjustment I was not ready for, and even though I was no longer living with my partner, I didn't sever all ties with him. He visited me occasionally, and so did I. I kept lingering in the broken cisterns of my past, and soon they broke open into a gaping pit.

While I was living with my brother, my nephew also came to live with us. After a while, a huge disagreement ensued, and we found ourselves estranged. My nephew and I had to move out. I had no idea what to do or where to go, so I slid into the familiar and took my nephew along. This time, I prayed harder than ever before and saw God's faithfulness manifested quickly. A friend was moving out of state and leaving her apartment because her mom had passed. She was not ready to give up the apartment, so she asked me to move in, which I gladly did. God was making a way for me, and I grabbed it with both hands. I didn't know what was ahead, but I believed God was working it out in my favor, so I stepped out in faith and moved.

This was a noticeable upgrade from where I was living before. I now had the space to spend quiet time with God and seek His will for me.

I became active in church, joined the women's ministry, and started serving. When we move in faith, God takes care of the rest. I was still going through traumatic moments, but God was doing His work. My family was still broken as there was no communication between us, and the pain of that was immense. I trusted in God for deliverance from what I was going through, and He delivered me.

It is essential for us to rest in God and let Him guide us. During this time, I rediscovered the Holy Spirit's companionship. As my faith in Christ grew, I observed how God took me from the pit of an ensnared relationship to the pinnacle of His divine providence. By then, my work visa was about to expire, but I wasn't afraid of what would happen because my faith in God had rekindled and now had a steady blaze. I knew that He would work it out and that He did. Not only was my visa renewed, but God used my CEO to initiate the filing process for me to secure my permanent residency.

I remembered having a conversation with God. I said, "God, I don't want to be here, but I believe you have a purpose for me here, and all things work together for good according to your words. I have already seen how you've been working; now, I'm asking that you grant me the privilege of being a legal resident in the US. I refuse to do it through any illegal means. Your words said, 'What does it profit a man to gain the whole world and lose his own soul,' and I'm not about to lose my soul for a green card. So, God, do what only You can and work it out. Thank you, and Amen." That was my prayer.

In the process, I've had many people present other options, such as getting married, since it was the easiest option, but I was at a place where I trusted God to divinely intervene. I trusted His guidance and timing, so I refused all other options. God did indeed work it out in His own time. I secured my green card faster than many people who came to the USA, even before me. I am so thankful to God for what He has done for me through my CEO (may his soul rest in peace). He transitioned eight months after I received my permanent residency. This broke my heart, and I still grieve his passing today. But God used him to deliver me from a significant pit. Despite the bumpy road and constant slipping and sliding in and out of my pits, God never gave up on me. He took me out of that abusive relationship pit once last time and poured debris in it so that I could not return to it. Our family has also reconciled; our relationship has been renewed, and we are closer today.

God has never failed any of His children, and He isn't about to start now. He has the perfect time for His blessings, breakthroughs, and benevolence. It doesn't matter your level of brokenness, how many times you have failed him, your situationships, or deep despair. Trust in God's timing. Accept His plan for your life, knowing that amid uncertainty and chaos, He is working everything out for good for those who love Him and are called according to His purpose.

Meet Marsha Gregg

Marsha D. Gregg is a highly acclimated professional in a multiplicity of areas. She is the founder and CEO of She Thrives Inc., an organization geared towards mentoring and serving women to help them identify and pursue their God-given purpose with their innate gifts through entrepreneurship and personal financial management. She is an author, speaker, a certified financial coach with Ramsey Solutions, and a recently appointed member of the advisory board at Mercy University.

Marsha's holds the position of Assistant Fiscal Officer with the most prominent non-profit childcare organization in Brooklyn, NY, USA. Additionally, she serves as a leader in various Ministries in her church. Marsha's personal journey, guided by her faith, has led her to pursue ministerial studies with the New York School of Ministry. Her passion lies in helping others, especially women, fulfill their divine purpose in this lifetime.

Connect with Marsha at: Facebook: marshaDgregg, Instagram: @Marsha_d_gregg, Twitter:@Marshadgregg, LinkedIn: linkedin.com/in/marshadgregg

CHAPTER 5

"This Sickness is not to End in Death!"

─────────────── 66 ───────────────

When Jesus received the message, He said,
This sickness is not to end in death; but it is
to honor God, and to promote His glory, that
the Son of God may be glorified through it.
John 11:4 (AMPC)

─────────────── 99 ───────────────

It was a typical day; the bright sun shone outside, and the school buses picked up children for another school day. I did the usual morning routine and got ready to take my son for his annual doctor's visit. I hurried him to the car and headed to the doctor. We made it just in time and were checked in. The nurse came and called Abdueli to take his vital signs and weigh him, and then we were asked to wait in the room for the doctor. When the doctor came, she started joking with him, saying that he was getting old since he was now in double digits; he had just turned 11. She then asked him to take off his shirt and touch his toes so she could check his spine. As he did this, something unusual popped out below his shoulder on the right side of his spine. The doctor asked him to bend one more time and called me to look and see if I noticed anything. When he bent over, I saw the large round thing protruding from his back. I had never noticed it before. My son said it did not hurt, but the doctor was very concerned.

The doctor gave us a referral to Boston Children's Hospital, one of the best children's hospitals in the world. Because of its popularity, getting an appointment can take up to a year. However, to our astonishment, we received a call from the doctor's office informing us that our son had an appointment in a week. While this was great news, it also left us with numerous questions concerning how serious his condition was. Securing such a prompt response to an appointment could be an indication that the problem was more urgent and complicated than we thought. We went to prayer as a family and did not share the situation with others. This was the beginning of digging the pit.

The day came, and my husband, son, and I took the one-hour drive to Boston Children's Hospital. When we arrived, we found the team ready and waiting for us. We went through registration, and immediately, they took Abdueli for X-rays and MRI, and we had to answer many questions. After five hours of going up and down, moving from one wing to the other, we went home, waiting for the results or a follow-up call.

After two days, we received a call from the hospital to return for more imaging tests. We went the next day, and another MRI and X-ray were performed. The doctors said they needed to reexamine the pictures to conclude their observations. Based on the hospital's reception, we knew whatever the team was seeing from the tests must be something big, and therefore, we prayerfully and patiently waited for the results. During this wait, we had sleepless nights. My husband and I would stay up discussing and asking what this could be, but most of the time, my husband was assuring me that God was able to calm me as he comforted me amid my uncontrollable sobbing. I remembered how I dreaded nighttime because once the children went to sleep, the fountain of my eyes would open. I would cry until morning, then clean up, get dressed, and take my son to one more specialist or doctor's office. I pleaded with God to help me take courage, but the more we waited, the more my stomach churned and recoiled.

As for my son, he only had two complaints: missing school and drinking the contrast fluid or "the glow-in-the-dark drink," as he called it. After five MRIs, we had a conference meeting with the doctors and other specialists who had been examining our son. During the meeting, they informed us that he had a tumor the size of an orange, and the mass had spread through the spine to the lung cavity. A biopsy would have to be done to determine if the tumor was cancerous. Hearing the word cancer, I felt nauseous and dizzy. I was sure I was going to pass out. I tried to keep my face straight while waiting for the doctors to finish their report.

The doctors said even if the tumor was not cancerous, based on the location and the size, the surgery was expected to be very complicated. The doctors warned us that various risks are involved whenever you touch the spine and the heart. They also related that there was a possibility of them removing part of his lung. The chances of surviving without major damage were slim; even if he survived, his recovery would take a long time. I started praying for God to take us through this road. I started imagining how our lives would be impacted as we cared for him. We would have to change jobs, or at least one of us would have to stay home and stop working.

I checked out of that meeting; my emotions were erratic. I thank God for my husband, who was calm and composed throughout the meeting. He was even able to ask questions and seek clarification.

I must admit that our faith was shaken and tested to the maximum. These are the times you can't help but ask God the "how" questions. How could God, who allowed me to experience bedrest for two months and kept the pregnancy against all odds, now let this happen? How could God, who performed a miracle for the birth of this child, now allow cancer to end his life so soon? How could He sanction this child to come home breathing on his own after being in the Neonatal Intensive Care Unit for two months and then allow this? The questions were endless. Our family felt helpless, and it felt as if all we could do was weep. And that is what we did. We wept so loud that the neighbors heard and came and joined, then friends heard and joined, and then church members and strangers heard and joined. We all joined and cried out to God. We had prayers from literally every angle of the earth. We received texts and calls from friends and strangers from different parts of the world. We received calls all day of assurance that there was a church praying, a group fasting, or an individual pleading on our son's behalf. These calls were our life support; they carried us through. We received encouragement, trusted God, and reminded ourselves that this disease was not unto death but for the glory of God.

The appointments were tiring; we were at the hospital almost daily for tests and meeting with various specialists advising the best treatment. Most of the appointments were on the cancer floor, and being there frequently triggered our emotions as well. Meeting parents and children travelling the same or worse made the voyage even more emotionally tiring. The team at the hospital wanted us to prepare for the worst. Therefore, my husband and I were assigned a counselor, a social worker, and a team that would oversee the planning of the chemotherapy schedule.

We were given a tour of the different facilities available at the hospital for parents who came for chemotherapy. I sometimes felt like I was in a bad dream; I had no appetite and spent most of my days crying. I was tired emotionally and physically. My body was weak, and my faith was growing weak as well. I could resonate with Mary and Martha as they waited for Jesus to come while their brother's health continued to deteriorate. My husband had an immense burden of holding himself up and holding the whole family. My son also started to get worried as he observed people coming to pray, encouraging us, and hearing the conversations over the phone about him. Then, the date came to do a biopsy. I remember it was an 8 am appointment. Since it was downtown Boston, we had to leave the house at 5:30 am to make it on time. We arrived at the hospital, and after paperwork, we went to the room to prepare for the surgery. The anesthesiologist came and explained to my son what he would do. Then, my son asked him if he would be able to wake up after the surgery. Even though the anesthesiologist assured him that he was going to be ok, I remember the first time I saw fear in my son's eyes. My heart broke as they wheeled him away.

A few hours later, the surgery was over, and it did not take long for my son to wake up. We left the hospital and went home to rest. I am not sure what was worse, all the run around we had done for three weeks or the waiting for the biopsy results. After one day, we received a call from the hospital, and the results came back negative. I remember being at work; I sprinted out of the office and went into the elevator to scream. I needed a good cry, the one where you had no shame about how your face looked. While crying, the pediatrician called. She was also crying, and by the sound of my voice, she just said, "You heard right?" Then she reminded me how I kept telling her that the God who had allowed the miraculous birth of this child would not put me to shame. And probably for the 10th time in that conversation, she said, "You must write a book." She will surely be among the first to receive a copy when this book is released.

The first hurdle had passed, and now we had to meet with the doctors to agree on the plan of how the tumor was going to be removed. By this time, I was emotionally drained. I thank God my husband was present because I just sat in those meetings and waited for them to end to ask him to explain what T-4 was.

The procedure was complicated, so it took a team of doctors to agree on the process. After three visits, we were given a date for the surgery. The groups that had been praying continued to pray for God to complete His miracle. We kept claiming and reminding God that the disease was a showcase of His power and glory.

The day of the surgery came, and we had a team of relatives and friends who accompanied us to the hospital. Some even travelled from out of state to be by our side and witness another miracle in the making. We occupied one section of the waiting room, and I counted fifteen people! My husband and I were overwhelmed with the love and support shown.

The surgery was scheduled for six to eight hours, and the doctors had informed us that the recovery would be at least three to four weeks before he was allowed to even return to school. At the waiting room, we took out our hymnals and started to sing hymns of praise, and in between, we gathered and prayed. It was a beautiful moment that I will never forget. I had so much peace, and my faith was recharged. If *all these people believed, why would I doubt it?* After one hour, the nurse came out of the surgical room and informed me and my husband that the surgery was going very well and the neurologist would be out soon to speak with us. As the nurse said, an hour later, the neurologist came and called my husband and informed us that things turned out to be very simple; nothing was as bad as they had anticipated, so the surgery should be done in another hour. We went back and informed the team. There were lots of tears of joy, and songs of praise rose.

At some point, I felt guilty about how we took over the waiting room. Thankfully, it was a good size room. As we were told, a little over one hour later, the nurse called my husband and me to a room to wait for the surgeon. In a little over three hours, the surgery was successful. The surgeon came to the room with a big smile and said, "I am not sure what happened, but once we opened him up and tried to pull the tumor, the whole thing just came out; we did not have to do any extra work." The process of removing the tumor was shorter than the process of preparing for the surgery.

My husband and I knew this was an answer to all the prayers. We thanked the doctor and left the room to bring the good news to the prayer team. There were more tears of joy and more prayers of thanksgiving. Indeed, without a doubt, God had proven that this sickness was not unto death but unto His glory. The nurse came and took us to the recovery room, which was big with a great view of Boston. Since my son was expected to be in a hospital for a while, he was given one of the best rooms on the floor. We gathered in the room and prayed together before separating. My husband and I and a few other people stayed and waited for my son to be fully awake. That was Friday when the surgery was done. Saturday, by noon, the doctor said he was doing very well and that if he could use the bathroom without a catheter, then on Sunday, they would discharge him. Everything was happening so fast and out of process that no explanation would make sense apart from giving God the glory for orchestrating all these plans.

Saturday at midnight, my son could use the bathroom on his own. The nurse smiled and said, "I guess you're determined to leave us." When the doctor came in the morning, he informed us that everything was well and our son would be discharged. I had such an emotional roller-coaster and was unsure how to handle all these events. I was overwhelmed by how God had favored my son. There is nothing special about my son or our family, but God chose my son to be the showcase for His glory.

I think about how there were many tombs around Lazarus' tomb, but Jesus called just Lazarus to come forth. And for that day, only Lazarus was resurrected. When we left the hospital, I was very emotional as we said goodbye to parents who were not sure how their journey was going to end. I kept asking God why Abdueli. What purpose do you have for him? Can we fulfill this purpose so that this miracle will be worthwhile? When we got home, my son was in bed for two weeks, and he went back to school. Even though he could not join the basketball team, he was happy to be in class again and resume his regular schedule.

I have asked myself questions that perhaps others have also asked themselves. Why did Jesus resurrect Lazarus but not John the Baptist? Wasn't John doing great things for the kingdom? I will never be able to answer such questions while I am here on earth, but one day, when I see Jesus's face, I shall have the answer. I also ask every time I see the scar on my son's back: why did God choose to spare his life this time? I will never be able to answer.

I am not sure what pit you are in right now, and I don't have a way to assure you that the outcome will be like my son's, but I know that God is faithful to those who call on Him and that He hears the prayers of those who cry out to Him. Our part is to pray and ask God to prepare us to receive the answer. There were many other times that the answer did not come the way I wanted, and my faith wavered. There are health challenges that my family is going through right now, and we do not know the end of it. However, we are reminded that His will is perfect, no matter how painful it may seem to our naked eyes.

We will never know when whatever sickness we experience will end in death or healing. For our son, his sickness was not unto death but unto the glory of God. Through this experience, our prayer lives changed because we experienced the power of prayer. Through this testimony, we pray you will find the courage to press on with prayer because only God understands His ways. Don't be discouraged, for you will never know when your breakthrough will be. Just persevere in prayer. The God who decided to resurrect Lazarus on that day or the God who saw fit to deliver my son from cancer is the same God who will deliver you from the dark pit you are in right now. Press on and keep your faith; remember, prayers have power.

Meet the Edna Eliamani

Edna Eliamani was born in Tanzania but currently resides in the United States. She is a fun, energetic, and camping fanatic. She has been involved in the children's ministry in the community and church for over 30 years. Edna has a heart for ministry and a passion for inspiring others through her words. She has dedicated her life to spreading the message of hope, love, and faith, touching the lives of many of her family, friends, and colleagues with her handwritten messages full of encouragement. Edna's journey has been of faith and perseverance, facing challenges with unwavering trust in God's plan.

This testimony reflects Edna's profound spiritual insights, offering readers a source of strength and inspiration in their walks of faith. Edna hopes that through her writing, she can continue impacting lives and uplifting souls by sharing God's love with the world through her stories.

CHAPTER 6

When Purpose Meets Connection

> 66
>
> *Trust in the Lord with all your heart, And lean not on your own understanding; In all your ways acknowledge Him, And He shall direct your paths.* **(Proverbs 3:5-6)**
>
> 99

The wisest person in the world was born out of unfavorable circumstances, yet despite his unsavory genesis, he emerged as a fountain of wisdom and inspiration throughout the generations. King Solomon (the son of David and Bathsheba) was a man who, despite being known for multiple wives and concubines, received one of God's most notable and enviable gifts—wisdom. When he started his journey as a king, we witnessed a mind-boggling yet divine-inspired verdict that spoke volumes of his intellectual capacity. This was the story of the two mothers who were feuding over ownership of living and dead babies. In one snap decision that can only be attributed to divine inspiration, he asked for the living child to be cut in half. Thus, history was written because the true mother wailed in agony for the potential impending doom of her child and requested that the other mother have him instead. King Solomon quickly discerned the authenticity of the mother through his calculated scheme, and justice was served.

Like Solomon's story, my first of three testimonies started with me making certain decisions that I can only ascribe to divine providence. It was in the Summer of 2012 when this testimony began. I was in the second semester of my first year of university. I was making my way home to Cambridge from a BBC One panel show, where I had to contribute a vote to decide if I felt the decisions of the UK parliament were helping the economy at that time. As I walked from the venue where this panel was hosted, I met another fellow university student who attended this event. While conversing, I noticed the arrival of an email for a business competition in my inbox.

The business competition was very reputable but was hardly known then because it was in its launching stages. I told this young man with whom I was conversing with immense conviction that I would apply to this competition. With much derision, he bade me good luck. Those who know me know that I relish a good challenge because the God I serve has brought me a long way, and I know with utmost confidence that if it were His will, He would grant me success in this venture.

When I got home, I combed through all the details of the email to fully grasp the task at hand. After much deliberation and careful consideration, I prayed fervently to God. I asked Him to provide me with a business plan to submit, as it was the main requirement to enter the competition. I had to fill out an application form and complete a business plan.

At this juncture, I had already studied business at both GCSE and A Level, and had some college modules. However, despite having all this knowledge, I still wanted to trust God in this process as, if I was successful, this could be a pivotal stepping stone for my future endeavors.

The competition I applied for was called "BBC Three's Be Your Own Boss" and was hosted by Richard Reed (one of the co-founders of Innocent Smoothies). Upon completing the application process, I patiently awaited the outcome and trusted my petition to God.

One day, while sitting in my bedroom in London (after returning home from my Easter break from university), I noticed a new email in my inbox. The only thing I saw was the word "successful." I was in complete awe of how God had allowed my application to pass this stage. Thousands had applied, but only 500 were selected for the next round. As God had gotten me this far, I felt impressed to ask Him to help me in this phase. I went on to the next stage, which involved pitching my business at an expo and using £100 of Richard Reed's money to make a return as great as possible.

Both tasks seemed too daunting to me initially because selling products was not a skill I had developed in the past, but I went forward enthusiastically. I set up a stand at my university and sold as many products as possible that I had purchased from the supermarket. To my amazement, I was able to incur a profit of around £400. Little did I know that this success would put what I regarded as a fickle business idea on the radar of those who hosted this competition.

After seemingly conquering this process, I presented my business idea to the expo with my eldest sister. I had this newfound confidence in God and felt nothing could be said or done to deter my path. My eldest sister noticed how significant my achievement was and not only commended me on how far I had come, but she was also astonished by the caliber of people I was exposed to and engaged with.

Before we even had a chance to enter the area where I had to present my business to an assessor, I was applauded for my company's efforts. Many expressed how excited they were about my business. This was astonishing because my business was only an idea, but their adulation confirmed that I could not take credit for this; all the praise and honor belonged to God and God alone.

As we walked into the expo, my enthusiasm plummeted. Looking around, I felt like all hope was lost when I saw another business idea that made mine look mundane. This business concept seemed so revolutionary that I thought the sign and the desk they provided me were a miserable attempt to pitch anything, let alone a fully-fledged business enterprise. However, my elder sister's zeal for me to meet Richard Reed and some of his business judges truly boosted my confidence and assured me that God was still at work.

We eventually got an interview with someone I would later meet in person again in 2023. Tim Campbell (the first winner of The Apprentice: A BBC TV Business series) gave me advice that, although simple, resonated with me until this very day. He said, "Your business idea is good, but you need credibility." I needed this sentence to affirm that one day, God would allow this plan to come to fruition. Unfortunately, I did not make it to the next round, but I was fully convinced that not being a qualified accountant would not deter me from implementing what God had started to place on my heart. A seed was planted, and as Charles Spurgeon says, "God is too good to be unkind, too wise to be mistaken; and when you cannot trace His hand, you can trust His heart."

From this encounter, I realized I was in a seed pit, and with God's nurturing care, I would bear great fruit in the future. I just needed to wait on Him and trust His plans for me. Shortly after God blessed me with my efforts with "BBC Three's Be Your Own Boss" between April and June 2012, I had another intriguing experience. I had recently returned from studying abroad in Malaysia between January and August 2013, and I no longer felt led to serve in my local church's youth department. I desired something greater. I sought the Lord in prayer again and told Him I wanted to be in some kind of ministry. I couldn't have possibly dreamt of what God had in store for me. It was the fifth anniversary of "Jesus and Ministries Bible Study," and a powerful and riveting sermon was delivered by a young man named Asher McKenzie. As he gave his altar call, I felt the Spirit pushing me to commit to serve, and I boldly accepted the task.

As I sat in a room with a large group of youth who had either accepted the call to be baptized or serve in a greater capacity, I wondered what this new ministry would require. I was excited about what could be birthed from this situation. A short while later, I found myself speaking to the SEC (South England Conference) Youth Director at the time about volunteering to help run programs with him, such as "Mission to the Cities," ushering at the annual SEC Camp Meeting, and putting together engaging programs to inspire young people to be drawn closer to God.

Before these experiences, I did not know what the South England Conference was. My exposure was limited, so I worked tirelessly in my local church to help the youth organize sports days, Bible studies, youth choir, and youth seminars on prophecy and Ellen White's writings.

As I found myself becoming more immersed in working with my local church conference for the youth department, I was presented with an opportunity to join a lay preaching course called HIT London. This course was previously unfamiliar to me, and I had a rudimentary understanding of how to preach based on what I had seen, as I was never taught. While I was genuinely terrified by the thought of working out of my comfort zone, I enjoyed meeting new people and finding out how to structure an expository sermon in a captivating way across all four areas of London with a campaign.

My first big challenge in this program was running my first campaign alongside a preaching colleague. My job was not only to preach and then be assessed on the spot, but I was also tasked with properly introducing my colleague. This task was made more daunting because I was asked to preach after the vesper service (a short feature that usually occurs at the closing of Sabbath services). As I listened to the feedback that I sounded more like a teacher than a preacher, I took it in strides as I earnestly desired to continue perfecting my craft because God was directing my path and not me.

As I matriculated through the HIT London program, I found myself preaching in an area close to Heathrow Airport. I could see the airplanes in full view as they took off to their destinations. In like manner, God was preparing me to take off in ministry. Despite the great distance I traveled to speak to this small congregation, I did not let anything deter me from preaching. I soon realized that I needed this sermon not just to confirm that this was my calling but was also God's way of teaching me that nothing good ever came easy. The sermon was entitled "There is a Purpose," it poetically summarized my entire journey throughout the year as it looked at the experience of Daniel, Shadrach, Meshach, and Abednego as outlined in the first chapter of Daniel. These godly men challenged King Nebuchadnezzar's direction and stuck to a diet of only vegetables and water for ten days. For this final effort for the program, I drew upon everything I had learned, from exegesis to biblical numerology. I explained the text in detail, expressing to the congregation that their purpose was rooted in the heart of God and that they needed to be unwavering in their faith.

As I returned to my university church for the final year of my studies, I received words of validation and confirmation in the AY (Adventist Youth) program. In this program, my course teacher publicly affirmed me and stated that I should be engaged to conduct Bible studies, sermons, and any other event that involved teaching and exhortation. In this instant,

I knew that something pulchritudinous would take place, even though I previously could not see how this process would come to fruition.

At the heights of my spiritual walk, I had moments of indiscretion that led to me falling off the path God had charted for me. Although it produced one of my most cherished gifts, I acknowledged that I had misrepresented God and had to bear the consequences. Like David, I had to seek God's pardon and accept the consequence of church censorship. This dire situation meant I had to relinquish my positions in church and make a recommitment. After going through my process of repentance, I reached out to someone I would today regard as a true inspiration and positive role model to re-establish my position as a youth lay preacher. Grace was extended, and they offered me various appointments for youth days across London. I would soon garner more and more experience and become so enthused by the process that I used my preaching ministry to share how God had carried me in the form of songs whenever I would appeal to the congregation.

This collision with my calling, how I fell from grace, and the forgiveness and pardon extended by God and the church both humbled and anchored my faith in Him. It was an arduous journey, but I learned that when we are in the pit of growth, the enemy will try to kill our purpose and thwart God's plan for our lives. Wherever and whenever I preached, many expressed that I was a motivation, and much credit was given to the preaching course I took, which even opened doors in my profession as an accountant, which I will begin to share in the subsequent testimony.

From around 16 years old, I always knew I wanted to be an accountant. However, as the finance sector is so vast, I first needed to study the subject at A Level to learn how I would do this. In my first couple of accounting classes, I felt a connection like that of a plug and socket. All the scintillating facts, figures, concepts, and foundations of accounting took root and made me enthused. I developed a hunger and thirst to learn everything possible in accounting. So, after completing my A Levels, I had to choose between embarking on a university course of study or seeking an apprenticeship. I decided to do the former because, unfortunately, I did not win the scholarship for the apprenticeship I had applied for.

As I studied for my accounting and finance degree, something kept telling me I needed to make my degree stand out. It was not enough just to complete a degree and work; I needed to have a memorable experience because I was among the last people to attend university before the tuition fees increased.

Due to the confidence I had developed in the lay preacher's course, I was inspired to do something brave and daring: to apply for the study abroad program, where I had to complete an application explaining why I wanted to study at another partner university. My confidence in Christ led me to believe that I could do all things through Christ (Philippians 4:13). I successfully applied and found myself spending the second semester of my second year in the beautiful country of Malaysia, where I have been able to find a church family that I connect with even to this day.

Upon returning, I dared to push the barrier further by taking a year out of my degree to learn how to apply my theoretical knowledge in an accounting firm where three partners taught me. After finishing my degree, I briefly worked for one of the partners until I found myself in my first post-university role after applying for almost a year.

You would think everything would be smooth sailing after this, but I found it quite challenging to transition from studying to working because my degree did not prepare me adequately. I worked in multiple start-up companies and was exposed to a wide range of experiences across the board. As I sought the coveted finance manager role, I checked in with trusted mentors to develop myself further in my career until I got to a role as a junior group accountant. However, a day before my 30th birthday, I received news I did not understand or anticipate. I was made redundant for the second time in my accounting career.

Most people during adversity tend to ask God questions, but it was during my bewilderment and frustration that I oddly felt at peace that God was going to come through. As I celebrated my 30th birthday, wondering how I was going to make ends meet, I saw a LinkedIn post where a friend from the past was seeking a finance manager. Despite my previous experiences with God, I felt incapable of doing this role.

However, with a mustard seed faith, I pursued the role with the help of my manager from my previous position. He prepared me for the entire interview process. Despite all the interviews and tests I had conquered, I was extremely nervous as I waited with bated breath after my second interview. I couldn't wait to hear, "You've got the job." Interestingly, I was at a complete loss for words when I heard them because, on paper, I was unqualified for the role. In this instance, I realized that God truly qualifies the unqualified.

I have waited on God many times, and I can genuinely say He has never failed me. Even when I didn't get what I wanted, I realized I got better than I initially anticipated. I now realize that God has been nurturing me in the pit of His hand and the pit of a seed as He prepared me for great things. A seed pit can be a dark, uncomfortable place, but as you are prepared to break forth roots, you will realize that the challenges and the pain are necessary parts of the process. I thank God for giving me these arduous experiences in life because they refined my character and built up an immeasurable amount of faith and trust in the

God of Abraham, Isaac, and Jacob! My friend, sometimes God has to break you to give you the blessings you truly desire, and only then can you appreciate His benevolent nature and bear fruit!

Meet Kingsley SYE Akrasi Jr

Kingsley SYE Akrasi Jr is a father to a handsome son called Micaiah (named after the prophet in the Bible who stood up to King Ahab) and a beautiful daughter called Maya (named after the civil rights activist Maya Angelou).

Kingsley is currently serving as the London chapter coordinator for Adventist Young Professionals, a youth lay preacher for the South England Conference of the Seventh-day Adventist Church for more than ten years (having preached in churches all over England) and the finance manager of Sweet Dee's Jerk Ltd (a business that is run by his friend from secondary school) with aspirations to one day have his own accounting firm and school and be an international motivational speaker.

He loves helping youths explore and understand their ability to serve God in whatever way God considers fit.

He hopes his testimony will help you discover your purpose, connect with God, and develop greater confidence in Him.

CHAPTER 7

Counselling With Jesus: Overcoming Fear and Staying Free

——— **"** ———

For God hath not given us the spirit of fear; but of power, and of love, and of a sound mind. (2 Timothy 5:7)

——— **"** ———

Fear, anxiety, stress, doubt, worry, and paranoia are all under the same umbrella. They have the same family name–LIES. Who is their father? The enemy of souls. Unfortunately, I allowed my mind to be home to this family for too long.

When we speak of the mind, we refer to our consciousness, intellectual activity, and thoughts. Our thoughts influence our choices and the emotions we experience daily. Our thoughts make up our character: "For as he thinketh in his heart, so is he..." (Proverbs 23:7). Our thoughts are not a separate entity from ourselves. We are what we think!

My mental health had been compromised twice before. My mind was plagued by the family of lies. How did I overcome them? "And ye shall know the truth, and the truth shall make you free" (John 8:32). In 2022, I experienced a mind battle for the third time, and this was when I decided it would be the very last.

This is a story of faith. God is real, and He is good. I didn't know God's presence and power were palpable and substantiative until my encounter with the enemy. Conversely, the enemy is also real and working overtime to captivate and destabilize our minds. What I have experienced is as real as the sun, the moon, and the words you are reading. The Spirit of God is alive and resolute about unshackling souls and transforming lives. I am a living testimony of His power.

The spiritual side of Christianity, as it relates to the battle of souls, is seldom shared and appears to be kept a secret. I want to break the ice and share my personal experience.

It started when I was young. I believed that God didn't love me, and that if I disobeyed His commandments, I would go to hell. I thought He was always waiting to punish me for every wrong deed. I knew there was heaven, and despite my perception of God, I still wanted to go there but thought, *"How could I get there if I am never doing the right thing?"*

As I got older, going out with friends and social events became an issue. My thoughts became irrational and paralyzing. If I was going out with my friends, I believed that something terrible was potentially going to happen to me. Or, if I went out and made it back home safely, this was a significant relief for me—a "phew" kind of moment. The thought I constantly lived by was, *"What if something terrible happens to me? "*

Fast forward to adulthood. I didn't know the truth (the Word of God), and I had already lived with irrational ways of thinking. Anything anyone said to me was accepted as truth. I stopped thinking for myself and allowed others to think for me. I would allow them to tell me what to do and dictate how to live my life. I listened and followed the instructions humankind gave me. Their negative thoughts and debilitating ways of reasoning also became my way of thinking and reasoning. God eventually revealed to me that this was the cause of my suffering.

What happened? I started noticing a change in my health in the year 2021. Fear and its siblings manifested themselves into symptoms. It started with my heart beating at a fast pace EVERY SINGLE day. It was going at least 150 beats per minute as if I had just run a 100m sprint. This caused severe chest pain on the left side of my chest, and I was constantly sweating. Each heartbeat felt like a knife stabbing me. I was in so much agony.

The negative thoughts also started to cause me to experience random electric shocks that ran throughout my entire body. These electrical shocks would also happen at night and shock me out of a deep sleep. I would be kept awake for the rest of the night and would cry in frustration, agony, and distress. I was suffering so severely. This went on for a while. I was scared that I might have a heart attack and experience a sudden death if I didn't get my heart checked out. So, I contacted my General Practitioner (GP), and they referred me to have some scans of my heart done, such as a 24-hour tape and an echocardiogram. I also made several visits to A & E (Accident and Emergency).

However, all the investigations came back normal. The doctors detected no abnormalities in my heart or blood tests. I was so surprised. I knew this was God was telling me that He had me covered.

October 2022 arrived, and I couldn't take the pain anymore. I had lost so much sleep because of my mind. By then, I had also developed severe breathing difficulties. So, I started searching the internet for medication to put an end to the torture. I researched Diazepam, Citalopram, and Propranolol. I liked the idea of being on Propranolol because it was designed to slow the heart rate, and Diazepam is like a tranquilizer; it would help me get some sleep.

One Friday night, I went to the nearest A&E. They prescribed Diazepam to help me get some sleep. I took the prescription, and while I waited in the hospital corridor, I felt the Holy Spirit telling me not to take the tablets. So, by faith, I left the hospital without getting the medications. I got in a cab and went home. I reached home around 1:30 am, and the first thing I did was rip the prescription to shreds and throw it away. I went to bed and, to my disappointment, could not sleep. I immediately regretted not getting the medication. I went to church the following day with zero sleep. My heart was working 10x harder because I had not rested. I could barely breathe.

Fast forward to one Saturday night (2 nights before traveling abroad), I was up all night and decided to call "111." I was begging them to deliver medication to help me sleep. I was so desperate. They said they only had morning appointments available to book me in for. Morning came, and I was waiting for the GP to call me so I could get my tablets. That morning, I cried to God on my bed and begged Him to help me. There was no structure to my prayer. It was just a cry for help.

After I had finished crying and praying, I heard a whisper. The voice said, "You can do it without the tablets..." This voice was external. I physically felt the breath of the voice hit my ears. It did not happen in my mind. It was not my thoughts. The voice was clear and sounded so pure. I knew God had spoken to me. The GP called me straight after my encounter with God. I let the phone ring, wrestling with myself. *"Should I answer it to get the tablets or honor what God just told me?"* "You can do it without the tablets." With good courage and faith, I ignored the call from the GP and decided to honor God.

I went on holiday and returned, but I didn't work on the advice God gave me. I didn't make any changes or efforts towards restoring my mind without tablets. "Even so faith, if it hath not works, is dead, being alone" (James 2:17). I came back, had a hernia repair surgery, and was confined to my room in additional pain for almost three months. Being by myself, bound to my bed most of the time, my thoughts started running out of control.

One Saturday morning, I watched an online sermon about controlling our thoughts. God was speaking to me again and I was quickly convicted to do something about my situation. So, I started to search on YouTube for testimonies on overcoming fear and anxiety. All testimonies said, "Read the Bible." But I had thought that I was already reading my Bible enough. Can you relate? Feeling as though you are doing enough as a Christian, and now you are being asked to do more?! I eventually humbled myself and took the advice.

First, I surrendered my life to God through faith in Jesus Christ in prayer. I gave up my will and asked God to take complete control over every area of my life. I got rid of everything in my life that had the slightest hint of dishonoring God, that tempted me to be disobedient, and everything that focused on worldly desires. I repented. I started my journey as a Christian all over again. I shifted my obedience and allegiance from mankind to giving complete loyalty and obedience to God. I also started to read the Bible more. I didn't just read, though; I BELIEVED what God was saying in His word. Anything that did not agree with the Word of God, I began to see clearly—that it was a LIE!

God started making over my entire mindset. He revealed that I needed to develop a mindset like His Son, Jesus Christ. "Let this mind be in you, which was also in Christ Jesus..." (Philippians 2:5). With every situation and person, I was counseled by the Spirit of God to change the way I thought about it or them. I was required to combat every single negative thought with Scripture. Jesus was counseling me through the Bible. Every new positive thought was given to me by the Holy Spirit. My job was to believe it and put it into action so that I would one day have a whole new mindset.

But my situation took a sudden turn for the worse. The distress in my mind eventually caused my stomach to malfunction. I was experiencing bloating and feeling full all the time. My stomach felt like it was going to explode. It felt like I had eaten, except I had not. As a result, eating meals became an issue. Feeling full meant I could not finish my meals. This went on for nine months. I lost significant weight. I went from 75kg down to 50kg. I became malnourished and bony in appearance. All I remember is the look on my family and friends' faces. They didn't know what to say. My whole appearance changed. I did not look like the Grace they knew.

I also became acquainted with hunger. Most nights, I went to bed hungry. Being hungry is painful, and I NEVER want to be hungry again! I cried so bad, but amid the storm, I chose to press on in faith. I decided to adopt the Adventist Health Message. I started reading Ministry of Healing by Ellen G White and began to live by the eight laws of health. By that time, I was already a vegan, but I was not eating wholesome meals. Vegan junk food was my diet. My situation demanded that I cut ALL junk food out and start cooking my meals. I was fighting for the restoration of my mind and fighting to not die of malnutrition.

Eventually, the issues with my mind and gut became too much to manage. I eventually crashed. I became severely weak, and I could barely speak or shower for 24-48 hours. I had to take five months off from work. I used this time to get better and become more useful. I spent a lot of time doing housework. The kitchen was the first place I would go in the morning. Sadly, I would have the most negative thoughts while standing at the sink. I would ruminate things from the past at the sink. I had no control. However, the Holy Spirit began His work and gave me the power to develop positive thoughts. I learned to affirm myself: "I enjoy domestic work." "I am grateful to have the strength to do this." "Thank You, Jesus, for the opportunity to clean."

"Do all things without murmurings and disputings:" (Philippians 2:14). Complaining is one of the biggest injuries to mental health. This is because it causes you to focus on what you don't have instead of what you do have. I started to replace this mindset with an attitude of gratitude. This was HARD WORK! If you have a fearful/negative mindset, being grateful is the last thing you want to do. I humbled myself eventually and was empowered by God to intentionally point out the good side of my tribulation.

"Take my yoke upon you, and learn of me; for I am meek and lowly in heart: and ye shall find rest unto your souls. For my yoke is easy, and my burden is light" (Matthew 11:29-30). In summary, this means to follow the example Christ left us. When you read about Jesus, you will see He did not give His attention to His struggles, difficulties, or petty situations. He cast all His cares to God and focused on displaying the love of God so that we might be saved. So, I started to learn to mentally let go and give my burdens to Jesus.

Not caring about something doesn't mean it's neglected. It means you stop putting value on the matter in your mind. It's the high value we place on situations, things, or people that results in anxiety, fear, stress, etc. If, for example, you are struggling financially but have faith in the provision of God, you can confidently say, "Oh well," to the matter. That's precisely what I started to do. If things were going wrong, I responded: "Oh well, Jesus. I give it to you." Naked faith in God will cause you to let go. Then you can rest and focus on doing all that is right and good in the Lord's sight so that it might be well with you (Deuteronomy 6:18).

As I consistently walked obedient to the instructions of the Holy Spirit, chains started falling off—spiritual chains. I could not see them, but I felt them falling off, like a chain coming off a bicycle. Each chain had a name. The first chain that fell off was fear. I kept a journal of some of the chains that fell off and how I felt.

"Dear God, today, I felt the chains of fear break loose. Now, I can walk through the Red Sea, which has been parted for me. Staying free from fear is a choice and a state of the mind. I am exercising this freedom. I know You will sharpen your mind. I'm free from fear. I'm free in the name of Jesus!"

Chains of fear, paranoia, stress, worry, and doubt all fell off one by one. Some took longer to fall off, depending on which ones I was most entangled with. My mind became clearer. It was like seeing through a clear glass. And every time a chain fell off, I felt lighter in weight. I felt like I was walking on air, almost like someone had taken a heavy load off my shoulders. Over time, I noticed my facial expressions changed, and I was smiling every day. I was happier to see people. I started looking forward to waking up. Going to bed, I would say, "God, I am excited for tomorrow." These are some of the results of developing a positive mindset.

Spiritual warfare is real. "For we wrestle not against flesh and blood...against the rulers of the darkness of this world, against spiritual wickedness in high places" (Ephesians 6:12). The enemy wants to keep anyone who loves God and is striving to be like Jesus in captivity. This battle is tough! I wanted to give up on God several times in the pit. I kept asking God: "What is it that you want from me?" and "When will I finally be able to do it without the tablets?

I think positively now about every situation. For every negative thought, I use Scripture to overcome it. I actively believe what God says about something or someone, not what the world or people say.

How am I staying free? I intentionally keep my mind focused on Jesus Christ. I do this by having active and living faith. Jesus remains in my frontal lobe, where all high cognitive functions occur. I control what I see, hear, wear, eat, do, and what I believe. Nobody does these things for me anymore. I also actively manage my thoughts daily. As a result, I am aware of almost all my thoughts. I catch the negative thoughts and use Scripture to kill them.

The chest pains and the fast heart rate have gone. I am free from electrical shocks jolting me out of my sleep. I don't know what it's like to lose out on sleep anymore. I no longer suffer from chronic bloating. I am eating in abundance and gaining weight. I now weigh 60kg. I am not on a single medication for the health conditions I had developed. Praise God! I should have been on Diazepam, Propranolol, and Buscopan for my mind and stomach issues. Today, my medicine is my faith in God, His word, and living the Health Message. I do my best to guard the avenues of my mind from lies and unfruitful content on the internet and in conversations. I'm not perfect but I do my best! This is how I am staying free.

As I wait in my pit of recovery and for the second coming of Christ, I am determined to keep my eyes fixed on the One who loves me with an everlasting love and wants me to have a sound mind and not a spirit of fear. I am soon entering the promised land where I will rest from the hard work. "...After that ye have suffered a while, make you perfect, stablish, strengthen, settle you" (1 Peter 5:10). I rejoice in the One who has given me peace. Glory be to God Almighty for what He has done and continues to do for me.

Meet Grace Owusu

Grace Owusu is a Ghanaian currently living in the United Kingdom. She identifies herself as a pilgrim patiently working, watching, and waiting for the return of her Lord and Savior, Jesus Christ. She is occupying until He comes as a registered nurse with over eight years of experience in the field.

After experiencing ill health from 2021 to 2023, she developed a significant interest in health reform and the health message disseminated by Ellen G. White, a co-founder of the Seventh-Day Adventist Church. She is passionate about studying nutrition and enjoys sharing her personal health journey with her family and friends. In support of her passion for healthy living, she is the director of the Health Ministries Department at her church and is a part of the plant-based community at her workplace.

In her spare time, Grace enjoys formulating creative pieces of writing and designing visually compelling flyers, posters, and logos for events, birthdays, and more. She now has a growing Graphic Design business called GraceCreates.

Her business page can be found on Instagram under the name gracecreates2024

Email Address: *gracecreates2024@outlook.com*

CHAPTER 8

When God Said "Go!" While The World Said "Stop!"

———— 66 ————

The Lord said to Shama, "Leave your country and the people of your family and go to the land that I will show you. I will cause you to become a great nation. I will bless you and make your name great, and you shall be a blessing. I will bless those who bless you, and I will curse him who curses you. And in you, all the families of the earth shall be blessed." So Shama departed as the Lord had spoken to her. ***Genesis 12:1-4 (Personalized version)***

———— 99 ————

HILETTE A. VIRGO

It was 2020. The epic year that many had awaited. For me, this was going to be the year of something exciting. I had just gotten into a relationship, and although it was long-distance, we had already begun making plans for our next visit. I would take a trip to Europe during the summer and visit his family and hometown. However, this was also the year I wanted to pursue schooling in the United States of America, where I had applied to pursue graduate studies before I had met him. Then, I lived in my home country, St. Lucia, and both desires were thousands of miles away, in opposite directions.

I decided to make this a matter of prayer to know where God was leading. Day and night, I mulled over plans. Should I abandon the thought of studying and focus on starting a family? The latter was the direction in which my heart felt led. But my head was still in turmoil, with my desire to follow my dream career looming in the background. I knew I was at the age where I should start writing my own family chapter and put school on the back burner. With that thought, I decided to prioritize my traveling plans to see my new-found love. Either way, 2020 was turning out to be a year of great things, a year that would be the start of "happily ever after."

Then the news hit. News about COVID-19 was spreading like wildfire, and everyone was in panic mode. But not me. COVID-19 was far away, affecting distant countries; it wouldn't interfere with my plans. I reasoned that it was an epidemic restricted to specific countries and would be over in a few months so I could continue my travel plans. Right? WRONG! Little by little, places began to shut down as the dreaded illness spread and became a pandemic. But I refused to give up hope on my exciting travel plans. Then, one day, my boyfriend suggested that we go our separate ways. After all, it was becoming evident that our meeting again was becoming impossible. My heart sank. I had thought this was "The One." At that point, reality hit so hard that it sent me reeling. The world was in disarray, and so was my heart. COVID-19 was not going away, and it was not getting better. I watched in trepidation as my plans shattered one by one.

Disappointed, I accepted that this love story was not God's plan for me. Hence, since I had to give up my travel plans and prospects of a new relationship, I could now focus on my initial plan, hoping this one would be successful. I had already been accepted to a university, and while I did not have the necessary finances to proceed, I was confident that God would provide a scholarship. I presumed that finding a scholarship would be easy, considering my excellent grades from previous studies.

Consequently, the upcoming months were filled with me searching and applying for scholarships and grants, anything that would help offset the significant figures that stared at me as the amount I had to show evidence of in my bank account to be granted a student visa. Before moving forward with this school idea, I decided to wait until I was assured some financial assistance, either from a scholarship or a job on campus. I dedicated my time to spending every waking hour searching. I emailed every person I now had contact with from the university and was informed that COVID-19 had caused many job opportunities to shut down. I prayed that God would show me this was His leading by helping me find some means of financial security. But as the time got closer, nothing seemed to change.

One day, I received a friend request from someone from Nigeria I did not know. After searching, I learned we were planning to do the same program. We quickly became friends, and I shared with her that I was trying to secure a job before continuing the onboarding process. However, she began encouraging me to move in faith, suggesting that when I arrived on campus, I would be able to find something. I countered that I did not think it wise to take such a risk, as I did not have money even to cover the first year's tuition, let alone other living expenses.

Furthermore, opportunities were limited due to COVID-19. She insisted that I push forward, sharing that she was in the same situation. I waited as close as I could to the deadline, and with no assistance in sight, I decided to commit the matter to the Lord and continue the process with the school, accepting their offer.

The next step was to go to Barbados to obtain a student visa. I inquired from a friend there whether the embassy was in operation and was informed they had been closed. They also did not know when they would reopen for business. Nonetheless, I gathered all the necessary documents for the visa process in the meantime, and continued to pray that if it were His will, I would be able to get my visa. The day following my inquiry, another friend, who had no idea of my plans, sent me a random article that read, "US Embassy Resumes Operation in Barbados." I could not believe my eyes! This was a sure sign to me that God was saying, "Go!"

With all the necessary documentation obtained, I ventured to find a ticket to Barbados. This was when I learned that the major inter-Caribbean flights had also stopped running. I prayed, called airports, and searched the internet for any sign of resumption of operation. Meanwhile, people asked, "Are you sure this is a good idea? We are in a pandemic, and America is the epicenter. Maybe you should postpone your school plans." I recounted the one sure sign I had received, which led me to believe God was with me through this journey. I assured them that God would work things out for me.

I eventually learned that two smaller airlines were flying to and from Barbados. The tickets were expensive, and a

COVID test, costing $100 US, was necessary. I prayed, "Lord, help me get an affordable flight to Barbados, and please provide a way that I would not have to get a COVID test." After making a variety of calls, I connected with a travel agent and, with the help of a family member, purchased the ticket. That day, I was informed that the COVID test mandate was lifted. Hallelujah!

To my amazement, the flight to Barbados had only two passengers. This seemed like God had scheduled it just for me. After a rigorous interview process, I was approved for my visa! A few days later, I prepared to leave Barbados. As I got to the counter to check in for my flight, the service agent queried, "Where is your COVID-19 test?" Taken aback, I explained that I was told that it was not required, to which she countered, "It was not required to come to Barbados, but it is required to get on a plane to St. Lucia." She shared some COVID testing sites I could go to for testing, stating that I would have to wait 24 hours to get the results.

Dismayed, I explained to her that I was unaware and had no family in Barbados and no money to get a test nor stay an extra night at the guesthouse. Unfazed, she assured me that this was the rule and that I could not board the aircraft without it. Disappointedly, I left the counter and called the taximan who had taken me to the airport, as I was staying at his guesthouse. As I waited for his arrival and to be brought to one of the testing sites, I phoned my parents to relay the news. They were equally disappointed but quickly resorted to praying about the situation, asking God to do a miracle. They assured me I should trust God and that everything would work out. They then decided to call the health department in St. Lucia, explaining that their "child," who went for her school visa in Barbados, was stranded there because she had not taken a COVID test and had no family in Barbados. They asked whether anything could be done. The individual promised to investigate it.

Meanwhile, I was on my way to the COVID testing site, a little discouraged that my prayer request to take a COVID test had gone unanswered.

While at the counter giving my information to the receptionist, I noticed my parents calling. I quickly answered and promised to contact them once I was done with the testing.

"Testing? What testing?" Mom enquired

"The COVID test so that I can get on the plane."

"You went to get a COVID test? We thought you were at the airport. We spoke to someone here who said she would try to see what she could do so you could be on your flight."

"Oh, really? Well, I was told I could not board without it, so I decided to get it done and will have to come home tomorrow."

With some displeasure in their voices, they hung up. I continued giving the receptionist my test information and then was directed to the testing room. While on my way there, I noticed a foreign number calling. When I answered, it was the service agent from the airport.

"Where are you? We have been paging you!" she said.

"I went to get the test done," I responded.

"Oh, we just got a call from St. Lucia stating that you would be permitted to get on the plane without it. But you must hurry; the plane will leave in half an hour. How far are you?"

Hearing this, I quickly asked the lady to cancel my testing request and ran out of the building, assuring the service agent that I was not too far from the airport. Fortunately, the driver was waiting for me, and I quickly hopped in the vehicle, informing him that we were going back to the airport and I had to be there to catch the flight, which was scheduled to leave in 30 minutes. On the way back, I gave the necessary information to the service agent over the phone to get my boarding pass issued. As soon as I got to the airport, I collected my boarding pass and was instructed to go quickly to the plane, as they were waiting for me to board to leave.

Thirty minutes later, we landed in St. Lucia.

Calling my parents from the airport and asking that they pick me up created a scene akin to that of Peter standing outside the disciples' door while they prayed for his deliverance, but not expecting him to be delivered and to be at the door:

"Hi. I'm at the airport. Come pick me up."

"At the airport? Which airport?"

"St. Lucia."

"You're in St. Lucia? But I thought you couldn't board the flight."

"I was permitted to. Please come for me, and I will explain everything."

You can imagine the joy and thanksgiving we felt to God on our way home as we related our versions of the story.

As my plans for school continued, the next step was to find lodging. I knew no one in Colorado. It was just a random state where I had seen the desired program. Following the advice from a friend, I looked up Adventist churches in Colorado. I reached out to a few via email but received no response. One day, I was impressed to look up one of the churches on Facebook. My search revealed two individuals I knew from St. Lucia, mother and daughter, who had visited the church. I reached out and learned that they lived in Colorado, that the mother was renting, and that I could rent there when I arrived. This was another sure sign to me that God was leading.

Two weeks after receiving my visa, I said goodbye to friends and family in St. Lucia and boarded a plane to Colorado, the land of the unknown. One day later, I arrived at the new place I would call home. I continued to spend time looking and applying for scholarships and jobs, but nothing promising showed up. There were many moments of despondency and discouragement, wondering whether I had made the right decision to come here without any sign of financial assistance. To make things worse, the new friend who had encouraged me to push forward had not been able to come, as her embassy was shut down. Many days, I felt alone in that foreign land. I never expected to find myself in this predicament. Had God abandoned me? I had believed He would have parted the sea of financial burden. I had moved in faith, but here I was, with no help in sight.

At the end of the first quarter, just when I thought I was at my wit's end, I received an email from someone from the school whom I had contacted concerning my situation. She shared with me how I could get some assistance with living expenses by participating in a particular program. I quickly shared my interest and received the necessary information. This allowed me to become connected with systems designed to assist struggling students. I was informed of a school pantry, told how I could access funds that could be used for books or living expenses, and received information about receiving free meals. They also told me I could apply for a job at the cafeteria. I was elated! I could only thank God for coming through again.

As I continued my studies over the next two years, I did not receive the scholarship or graduate assistance job that I wanted. However, I was able to receive assistance from friends and family, which spoke more volumes about their love for me and willingness to support me than I would have ever known had I received a scholarship. I was also required to work several jobs, sometimes five at a time, to make the necessary money to cover my expenses.

I studied. I ran to catch and sometimes missed the bus. I rode my scooter through snowy and icy days. I waited in the pit of loneliness and despair. I often envied my classmates, who seemed to have it so easy. I was the only Christian, non-American, and black student in our class. Some days, I cried as I walked alone, realizing how difficult and lonesome this journey was. But I pushed through, reminding myself that this was only for a moment. Many times, just as it was time to meet a financial deadline, I would receive money or information just then to help me get through that season. Step by step, I was able to make it through.

Two years after my journey to America began, it was time for graduation. I paid my final fees and breathed a sigh of joyful relief. God had come through, and I finally saw the finish line. I had made it out of my pit. It was only then, during that final quarter, that I learned that while I had been toiling to pay my way through school and assuming that all my colleagues were wealthy, not having to struggle, I discovered that they all had school loans that they needed to repay! They, in turn, were impressed to learn that I was paying my school fees while attending school all this time, and I had the chance to testify of God's providence! God had me nestled in the pit of His hand all this time. He permitted two years of discomfort to grant me years of subsequent freedom.

On June 10, 2022, on my sister, who had supported me throughout this journey birthday, I walked down the aisle in my graduation gown to receive my diploma debt-free. I fought a good fight and finished my course with a 4.0 GPA. I have grown stamina and resilience through this process and built spiritual and emotional muscles. Even though my prayer was not answered as I had hoped, God had proven His faithfulness, and I was proud of what God and I had accomplished. Furthermore, when my friend from Nigeria was finally able to join a year and a half after I had arrived, she was privy to all the information I had gathered, thereby not needing to suffer as much as I did.

My journey with God continued with me having to find a job, and He led me to another state to get it in the field I desired, with a company willing to help me with what I needed to work successfully in this country.

I now await what God has in store now that this schooling season is over. My faith is stronger, and I now know that if He takes me to it, He will take me through it. I trust His promise to bless me and cause me to be a blessing in this country, and I can't wait to see where He will lead next.

Meet Shama Felix

Shama Felix is known for her friendliness, ambition, wit, and determination. She was born and raised on the Caribbean Island of St. Lucia and now resides in the USA. Shama is an Early Childhood Special Educator by profession and is privileged to support families of children with disabilities and developmental delays. Shama is involved in various ministries and continually seeks ways to serve and bless others. She is part of the prison ministries with the Washington conference, where she ministers to incarcerated women, sharing messages of hope and God's love.

Shama serves as the Young Adults leader at her church and is also part of the praise and worship team. Shama leads a book club geared towards single SDAs, allowing individuals to read and discuss various topics about having healthy Christ-centered relationships.

Shama enjoys playing the piano, singing, playing games with friends, and engaging in thought-provoking discussions (especially about the Bible) when she is not busy with all her other pursuits. She loves traveling and going on adventurous excursions. She is passionate about helping others and seeks to make the world better, one person at a time.

CHAPTER 9

Finding Solace in the Pit of Grief & Loss

---- **"** ----

For the grave cannot praise you, death cannot sing your praise; those who go down to the pit cannot hope for your faithfulness. (Isaiah 38:18 NIV)

---- **"** ----

Grief and loss, like joy and laughter, are natural to our human experience. If we live long enough, we will all experience losing loved ones, close friends, and people we have associated with because "death is as natural as birth." Some people have had to drink from the bitter cup of grief and feel the acidic liquid course through the veins of their souls, tearing at the arteries of their hearts and piercing their stomach walls multiple times in their lifetime.

Unfortunately, I am one of those people. I have felt the sharp pangs of grief ripping my heart to shred too many times for comfort. I have been thrust into the vicious, dark pit of grief and bereavement, languishing and seeking solace and comfort from the One who knows my heart's sorrow.

My first encounter with losing a loved one was when I was age 7 or 8 years old. My dear Auntie Muffi, my father's sister, passed away and broke my little heart. It took me a while to process the fact that she was gone, and I would never see her again, even though she had battled for months with what they speculated to be cancer. I couldn't describe the pain I felt when I tried to process that I would no longer hear her soft, gentle voice or behold her lovely face. She was someone I cherished and was also loved by my family.

Aunt Muffi had resided in a different community, and I valued every opportunity to visit her. I loved her company and enjoyed watching her make textile masterpieces with her skillful hands. She was an expert dressmaker who tailored all my school uniforms. We'd engage in small chats during our visits, and her serene demeanor always impacted me positively. As her health deteriorated, I earnestly prayed for her recovery, but regrettably, her illness prevailed, leading to her death.

The day of her funeral proved perplexing to my little mind as I gazed at her remains resting in the casket. Questions arose within me; I wondered if she could perceive the proceedings and grasp that this was our final farewell and that she was destined to be laid beneath the ground. The realization that her physical presence would forever vanish, that our interactions would cease, weighed heavily on my mind as the tears spilled down my cheeks.

That night, my rest was disrupted by anxiety and restlessness. I found myself drenched in sweat, my mind racing. I became intensely fixated on the notion that my departed aunt would manifest herself in the darkness. This was influenced by snippets of conversations I had overheard. My older relatives and neighbors claimed that the deceased could return on the third day to visit those closest to them. This stirred a mix of terror and anticipation. I imagined her making her rounds among her children, siblings, and, eventually, myself. Fear of the unknown gripped me, which I later discovered was rooted in misunderstanding.

As time passed, I gradually comprehended that our loved ones and those who departed were no longer capable of thinking, breathing, or existing in any form. As I got older and had a more profound understanding of the Bible, I understood and embraced the truth that the dead knows nothing, as expressed in Ecclesiastes 9:5. Yet, my aunt's passing left a lasting impact, instilling in me a deep fear of death that affected my perspective and interactions with mortality for years.

The realization had dawned upon me that life held no guarantees for any of us. Regrettably, I would go on to experience the loss of numerous other family members and exceptionally dear friends in manners I could never have anticipated. Unlike many other life incidences that, with constant recurrence, developed immunity, I never quite got accustomed or became less vulnerable to death's impact. In fact, with every loss, I found myself thrust deeper into the grief pit, fighting desperately to stay afloat. They have all left an imprint on my heart, and many have haunted me for years.

An incident from childhood remains etched in my memory, standing vivid and fresh as if it happened yesterday. One evening, the distant wail of sirens gradually grew louder, drawing our attention and concern. As the sound approached, my family and I watched as police vehicles and ambulances hurtled by, triggering a collective sense of unease and uncertainty. The prevailing tension was palpable as we looked at each other, wondering what was happening. Where were these emergency vehicles headed?

As time passed, we learned the heartbreaking truth. We would have never guessed that the sirens were responding to and heralding the demise of two young souls, our cousins. They had met a tragically gruesome fate. The ages of these innocent victims were very tender; one stood at merely five years, while the other was between ten and eleven years. The shocking news rocked our community, leaving us in deep sorrow. I can still hear the wails of my relatives as we struggled to come to terms with the magnanimity of the situation. How could this happen? Why?

This dreadful incident was confirmation that my life would never be the same. The aftermath of that day cast a shadow, altering my life and leaving a lasting impact on my experiences and perceptions. I was marred and scarred by this traumatic event, which left me fearing for my life and those of my siblings throughout my childhood years. Who would go next? This question haunted my psyche like a horror movie.

There was another incident that occurred in our community that slammed me against the wall of my grief pit, leaving me grappling for air. A girl around the same age as I was at the time, about ten years old or so, was found dead, wrapped in plastic. Evidence pointed to the horrifying fact that she was raped and left for dead. This is yet another painful memory that haunts my mind. I can recall attending the funeral with crystal clarity, and the image of the dress I wore stands out distinctly—a white, airy dress with a puffy design. The contrast between the innocent, youthful elegance of my attire and the solemnity of the occasion is a striking reflection of the emotions surrounding that moment.

I can recall the sequence of events that unfolded on that day. After departing from church that Sunday evening, our journey led us to the Bottom Road Seventh-Day Adventist Church, where the somber funeral service took place. The transition from the church service to the funeral venue captured the shift from a place of worship to a place of immense mourning. I walked up to the casket and looked at this beautiful little girl lying breathless in her casket as if she were sleeping.

During that time, many questions swirled through my mind. I was overwhelmed with confusion and felt a sharp pain slicing through my heart. Why were so many innocent children meeting such tragic ends? What circumstances could justify the cruel fate that befell them? The weight of these unanswerable questions left me deeply traumatized, their echoes resounding through the years that followed.

As time marched on, the trauma I carried with me intensified, leaving a lasting mark on my psyche. The impact of those past events manifested in unexpected ways, especially after I became a parent myself. The responsibilities of caring for my daughter and niece awakened dormant triggers, evoking a fierce sense of protectiveness that, at times, bordered on overzealousness. The memories of those lost young lives served as a haunting reminder of the fragility of innocence and the need to shield and nurture those entrusted to my care.

This heightened vigilance became a coping mechanism, born from a place of profound empathy and the desire to protect the next generation from the harrowing experiences that had marked my past.

As the years advanced, a disheartening pattern emerged— many of my male cousins, with whom I had shared my formative years, met untimely demise. The weight of these losses was a constant presence, an unending sorrow that gnawed at my heart. Witnessing the premature passing of these young souls, brimming with potential and aspirations for a bright future, was an agonizing blow. The cruel irony lay in their lives being cut short before they could even explore the opportunities ahead.

The news of each cousin's passing was like a succession of emotional blows, leaving me grappling with an assembly of conflicting emotions. Numbness, anger, sorrow, and confusion became familiar companions as I struggled to make sense of the relentless string of tragedies. The stark reality of death, particularly when it touched those so close to me, proved an overwhelming concept to reconcile with. These were the very same kids I had grown up alongside. We shared countless experiences of play, mischief, camaraderie, and every imaginary emotion. Our bonds were strengthened through laughter, tears, challenges, and triumphs.

In the face of this ceaseless barrage of loss, I found myself struggling with the weight of life's uncertainties. I made several attempts to push these agonizing realities aside and to suppress the memories that haunted me, but this proved futile. They became an inseparable part of my being, a heavy burden that shaped my perspective on existence. They left a mark on my soul and held me captive for years.

As if things couldn't have become more challenging, I decided to unwind outdoors on a crisp afternoon with some family members. Being in my third trimester of pregnancy, my belly had swollen considerably, and it was becoming increasingly difficult for me to move around. Amid this peaceful moment, I got a text from my child's father. He informed me that he would visit later after finishing some tasks. He had performed at a crusade the night before and had to pack up and move the musical instruments to their storage place.

As time passed, I didn't receive any further updates from him. I assumed he was still occupied with his work, so I didn't make any attempts to call him. A few minutes later, I noticed my cousin's boyfriend approaching us, but he appeared visibly frightened. He took out his phone, glanced at me, and continued walking in our direction.

One of my aunts approached him and inquired if he was okay. He blurted out the shocking news that our cousin, who had a band, had been shot, and my child's father was dead.

My initial response was, "What?" Hearing my response, he hastily changed his statement, suggesting that our cousin had been shot, but they weren't sure of my child's father's whereabouts, so there was a chance he might be okay. However, I couldn't believe his words because his statement had changed too swiftly. Overcome with grief, I cried out, "Oh God, he's dead."

My mother asked if I wanted to go to the scene, and I nodded in agreement. As we made our way there, we received the horrifying news that the car was now on fire, and it was deemed unsafe for us to approach the crime scene. Instead, we headed to a nearby hospital where they said my cousin was being treated, hoping that we would see the man I loved and the father of my child there.

Upon arriving at the hospital, I noticed a large crowd, and their expressions told me something was wrong. I was led to where my cousin was, and that's when the harsh reality hit me: The man I loved was dead. It was at the hospital that we learned he was still in the car, which was engulfed in flames. His body was burning while we passed the turnoff that led to the scene. Only God knew the depth of my anguish. I fell to my knees and screamed in agony. At that moment, I felt my life could not get any worse. I wondered about the purpose of it all, but the one reason I found to continue fighting was the child I was carrying inside of me. The devastation, numbness, and anger I felt were overwhelming.

So many questions were swirling in my mind, yet there were so few answers to provide any solace.

Revelation 21:4 (NIV):" 'He will wipe every tear from their eyes. There will be no more death or mourning or crying or pain, for the old order of things has passed away.

Grief has carved one of the deepest pits in my life's journey. There are moments when it feels like I'm emerging from its depths, only to be thrust back in, tumbling and jolting against the harsh surfaces of yet another loss. In my recently published book, *Inspired to Keep Pressing*, I wrote about a dear friend, a beautiful soul who was like a sister to me. I recently learned of her passing, and it broke my heart. I can't count how many times death has ripped my heart apart. I haven't shed a tear yet because I'm still in disbelief. You'd think that after losing so many people, it wouldn't hit so hard, but it breaks my heart every time someone I love dies.

The truth is no one ever gets used to losing someone dear; we simply learn how to live with it day by day.

My heart has borne this colossal burden for years. Sometimes, I am overcome with grief and anguish, but I somehow find solace only in God, who has remained the sole constant in my tumultuous existence. I amaze myself that I can still find comfort even with these avalanches of intense hurt and pain. I can only credit it to God's magnanimous grace. In Him, I find a refuge where I can fall when my strength fails. I cling to the hope that one day, death will meet its end. And on that day, all my tears will be wiped away, for death itself will be no more.

For those writhing in the pits of grief and despair, find refuge in the One who conquered death. Find peace in the One who knows our deepest pain. There are days when I feel the mountain of grief looming over my soul, but as I feed upon the word of God and breathe a prayer call for rescue, I find solace in these words:

*So do not fear, for I am with you; do not be dismayed, for I am your God. I will strengthen you and help you; I will uphold you with my righteous right hand. **(Isaiah 41:10 NIV)***

Meet Serena Rowe

Serena Rowe is blessed with the gift of singing, which she passionately utilizes whenever the opportunity arises. She is a songwriter, and author of her recently published book Inspired to Keep Pressing. She has also co-authored Waiting in the Pit 1 & 2. Serena possesses a creative eye, excelling as a graphic, website designer and a video editor.

Actively engaged in spreading the gospel, Serena makes herself available for ministry wherever the Lord leads. Presently, Serena ministers at various churches upon request.

Beyond her musical and ministry pursuits, Serena has volunteered at various organizations, earning recognition for her community service and advocacy work. Acknowledged by the Municipal Council of The City of Paterson, New Jersey, and the Mayor of Jersey City, Serena has received certificates of appreciation for her graphic design skills in city events.

Serena expresses an unwavering commitment to follow God wherever He leads.

www.serenaroweministries.org
Instagram: Seri_songbird
YouTube: Serena Rowe Ministries

CHAPTER 10

God's Relentless and Satisfying Love

---- 66 ----

He brought me up also out of a horrible pit, out of the miry clay, and set my feet upon a rock, and established my steps. (Psalm 40:2)

---- 99 ----

I remember feeling unwelcomed as the youngest and only girl of five children. I was named by and after my father, who really wanted a fifth boy—that is how I got the name Toni. My dad hosted many parties at our house, so people often came and went. Some saw me as an easy target for the sexual abuse, and I eventually experienced different men outside of the family between the ages of nine and 14.

I viewed femininity as a weakness and felt like a permanent target for more sexual abuse. Men seemed to have all the power, and I didn't like being vulnerable. On the other hand, my brothers seemed stronger, happier, and able to protect themselves. I wanted to be just like them.

I did not feel safe as a female and wanted to hide from being desired by men. I became so deeply depressed that I tried to take my life by overdosing. It didn't work, and the depression didn't go away. I was desperate to be held, loved, and cherished, not to be sexually abused and discarded like trash. I hated being a girl!

My loving great-grandmother's voice would echo in my thoughts, even though I did not see her often because she lived so far away. She consistently told me that "Jesus loves you" whenever I visited her. Although I didn't know much about God back then, those words comforted me during difficult times.

I left home as quickly as I could. Conflicted about my identity and trying to please everyone, I got married, joined a church, and got pregnant with my son. Even though I tried everything I knew to make it work, I still felt unsafe with my husband because he was a man. I struggled immensely with Major Depressive Disorder, anxiety, and PTSD with constant triggers from unresolved childhood abuse.

My husband's touch and glances reminded me of the men who abused me. His behaviors and actions were loving, caring, and healthy, but my brain was in a constant fight-or-flight mode. Anxiety and fear were my constant companions.

It was challenging to raise my son and deal with feeling empty and hopeless. I craved acceptance and affection from both parents, especially my mom. I realized that I struggled with being emotionally available to my son, just like my mother had struggled with me. I would imagine my mom being affectionate with me, but I knew she was still closed off emotionally. So, I started having fantasies of being emotionally and physically intimate with women.

I was needy and felt like I could never get enough affection. The devil suggested that if I were to live with a woman like how I lived with my husband all these years, I would get all the "safe" love and affection I wanted. My heart leaped in excitement! I decided to leave my husband and son and ran into the gay culture. I expected to leave the feelings of neglect, being unseen and unheard behind, and instead experience love, safety, and acceptance. Knowing that comfort from a person wouldn't heal the sexual trauma and emotional neglect I suffered, I decided I would eventually still take my life, but not before I experienced living with a woman.

I divorced my husband and married a woman.

Finally, I felt more in control of my circumstances. I still didn't think anyone had the capacity or desire to understand the depths of my pain. I also knew God would disapprove of my new lifestyle choices and potentially use my Christian friends to confront me about them. I still felt unsafe, but dressing as a man offered me the protection that I longed for all my life. The temptation to get a man's haircut, tattoos, and dress more masculine eventually overwhelmed me, and I gave in. I bought male clothing to feel "transformed" by the confidence and safety of living outwardly like a man.

Then, one day, my son confronted me about the changes in my appearance. I responded, "I'm not dressing like a man; I'm just dressing 'comfortably.'"

"C'mon mom," he said. "I can tell you want to be a man."

At that moment, I knew my response was a failure; even my son knew the truth! His compassion and love were never without question, and it broke my heart to disappoint him. It bothered me that I was confusing him with my delusion. Suddenly, I became aware that I was only deceiving myself.

I had a hard time accepting who God created me to be. He spoke clearly through my son, and I felt convicted about my appearance. It was as if God Himself were saying, "I see you, I love you, and I will protect you." Feeling comfortable with my femininity was a process, but in that moment, I had an indescribable desire for women's clothing like never before!

God started reminding me of His promises, laws, and abilities— how I could trust Him and how He still cared for me. He won me over with His relentless compassion and loving kindness. I was so amazed that I wasn't far from His love and mercy amid my sins.

As I claimed Christ's forgiveness, I found it easier to forgive my parents, brothers, and those who had abused me. What a relief to let go of all that pain! I invited God to close the door to my relationship with my ex-partner because I knew I couldn't do it on my own—and He did it. We separated within two weeks, and our divorce was final in two months!

I was excited to leave the lesbian life behind, but I was terrified to be alone. As I tried and tested Jesus, I realized I could trust Him more and more; He started addressing my pain at a gentle pace that I could handle. I wasn't free of making mistakes, but I still cooperated with Him one step at a time. His understanding of all my choices drew me in further. He never condemned me; He only wanted to heal and love me!

God affirmed that He not only loves other people, but He loves me too, even when I was a lesbian and hopelessly walked away from Him and my family! As I fell in love with and gave Him my heart, I followed His lead to begin my healing journey. There were many things from my childhood trauma that needed addressing, and He would bring truth to shut down every lie I believed. He also revealed how He was with me and provided for me through the traumatic experiences, like when He offered His gentle and reassuring love for me through my great-grandmother.

I realized that the One who created me ultimately knows how to satisfy me even more than I do! I also learned that I was genuinely seeking HIS love, acceptance, and safety the whole time. The God of the universe wanted to not only deliver me from the pit of lies, delusion, and entrapment but also shower me with His presence, love, and compassion! It wasn't easy initially to let Him into my heart, but it was life-changing when I did! The more I understood who He made me to be, the more courageous I felt being single.

Being close to Him set me free from dependence on people to complete me because I am already complete in Him. Many verses confirming my identity in Him moved from mere head knowledge into my heart, including *Psalm 40:2. I was in a miry pit, a dark, dreary place waiting for years to be rescued.*

Working out my inner healing journey with God, I can now see the beauty and blessing in my painful life experiences. He is helping me to actively witness and understand many core truths about my life and how they are integral to His plan. The greatest among these core truths is the reason why I was born female within my particular family dynamic and why I gave birth to my son. My family trauma led me to seek God for myself. He then used my son, a male I love and trust, to show His unconditional love for me. Otherwise, I wouldn't have felt comfortable trusting or desiring to get close to God.

After experiencing numerous breakthroughs and intimacy with God, I have brand new opportunities to lend an ear, console, and encourage others who have experienced trauma. It is a true blessing to have my pain transformed into purpose! God continues to bring healing and restoration into my life. Each day, He helps me walk out the calling He put on my life from the beginning: the gift of encouraging others. I pray to continue cooperating with Him as He genuinely loves me and can be trusted.

Written by Toni John
Georgia, USA

Meet Toni John

Toni John is originally from New York. She now resides in Georgia, USA. With a heart dedicated to lifting up leaders in prayer and sharing the message of Jesus Christ with the broken-hearted, Toni is on a mission to spread love and hope to those in need. As a devoted mother to a teenage son, she cherishes their time playing basketball and growing in their faith together.

Toni's creative spirit shines through in her love for writing poetry and crafting encouraging cards. Currently, she is pouring her heart into a book of poems that encapsulates her powerful testimony and is in the process of launching a Coaching Ministry to inspire and uplift others in their journey with Christ.

CHAPTER 11

Ted Talks Rejection

----- **"** -----

The stone which the builders rejected is become the head of the corner: This is the Lord's doing, and it is marvellous in our eyes? (Mark 12:10-11)

----- **"** -----

Rejection is not a unique phenomenon; we all have experienced and have had to deal with it in some way or form. My story is about how I have dealt with it and its long-lasting effect on me.

When did it all start? Let's go back to the worst day of my life.

There I was, feeling comfy with no care in the world. I felt secure and contented with life. Then suddenly, my world turned upside down. I was shocked and dazed. I couldn't figure out what was going on. I tried to ask for help but could not speak. I could not focus on anything. I felt cold and weak and in complete distress. Then suddenly, I realized I could not breathe. My distress must have been apparent as there were people around me, and one of them hit me! I wasn't sure if this was an attempt to get my attention or if someone was taking advantage of my predicament. At this point, I could take no more and responded the only way I could in the circumstances. I broke down and cried hard and loud. Then, out of nowhere, my mother appeared. She held and comforted me, and then everything seemed good. So, this is what it is like to be born. Sorry, did I say it was the worst day of my life? I meant the first day of my life.

From the moment I was expelled from the womb, I was thrust into struggle and discomfort, hence the expression of tears. By all indications, through science and pure observation, babies cry at birth because they are shocked by the new environment. If they do not cry, usually it's because their air passages are blocked or they are having respiratory challenges, and so the medical attendants will slap or inflict pain to have the baby cry. Therefore, as we enter the pit of life, our first response is tears. For some, the entry into the pit was sudden and overwhelming; for me, it was a slower process, like stepping into sinking sand.

I have been conscious of pain and discomfort from an early age. I have two distinct memories from early childhood, around two years old, that I have been unable to shake. The first memory is waking up, seeing sausages on a plate, and going back to sleep, but when I re-awoke, the sausages were gone. This happened several times. On the last occasion, I climbed out of my cot through the gap from the missing pole (large enough to allow me to climb in and out) and ate the irresistible sausages. Another memory is waking up in the morning, crawling to the top of the stairs to listen to my mother and aunty conversing in the kitchen. Once I heard the familiar tones, I would return to my cot.

It is said that moments of trauma can be totally forgotten or remembered, sometimes subliminally forever. So why are these memories so embedded in my mind?

"Ye shall know the truth, and the truth shall make you free" (John 8:32).

The sausages were my brother's breakfast, set out each morning until that one day when I ate them. From that tender age, I was exposed to neglect and had to learn to fend for myself. My babysitter had at least on one occasion, and perhaps many, as far as it is known, left me alone for what may have been hours. This came to light when she was held up while returning to look after me. It was discovered when my brother and cousin returned home from school to find me in a state of distress, crying, hungry, and in need of a nappy change. Is it any wonder why hearing voices was so important and why those sausages were so tempting? This was probably my first experience of being rejected, more accurately, being abandoned. Abandonment and rejection are similar, as abandonment involves rejection.

I am a middle child, and sadly, I have suffered from middle child syndrome as I have felt the pangs of neglect and inequality. For a while, I was the newcomer, the baby of the family, and was favored with all the benefits that come with it, until the day I was unceremoniously replaced as the baby by a new baby sibling. I now had no title. I was not the oldest and no longer the baby. I was in an in-between land, left to contemplate my place in the universe.

However, I experienced a whole period of being liked and admired. Apparently, I was cute, with an afro and a passing resemblance to another afro-haired youngster from a child pop group who was very popular at the time, but my teeth were not great to look at. It became my reason for keeping my mouth closed for most of my childhood and early adult life.

I was laughed at, ridiculed, teased, and became an instant target for everyone. I would hardly speak to anyone if it could be helped. Thus, I suffered from insecurities and rejection from early in my life. I started becoming shy and adopted a posture of invisibility as best as possible. If someone asked me a question, as soon as I tried to answer, I would be asked, "What's wrong with your teeth?" Hence, I tried to speak without opening my mouth, which consequently led me to speak very quietly and become pretty shy and withdrawn as I hid in my pit of shame.

Despite my shyness and insecurities, I always had a curious mind and a very active imagination, which probably didn't help me stay out of sight. Because I liked observing things, it wasn't easy to keep under the radar, but I did my best to remain inconspicuous. The last thing I desired was to be the center of attention. This meant I kept all my emotions, opinions, and creative ideas in check.

As I got older, I perfected my ability to stay unnoticed. No one could tell anything about me without getting to know me first, and this was next to impossible because I kept everyone at arm's length. Of course, it just meant more rejection. Who wants to hang around someone who displays the characteristics of a loner or is not friendly? And thus, I marinated in my lonesome pit.

If I could relate all my experiences of rejection, it would take up the entire content of this book. However, since I have only one chapter at my disposal, I will stick to the general theme. I have been touring this pit all my life, and as my title reads, I could give several "TED Talks" on the subject. Anyhow, let's keep it concise.

One of the biggest rejections I experienced as a teen caused me to miss a few weeks at the beginning of high school. When I returned, I found that most of the friendship bonds had been established already, and I had not made any friends. My classmates questioned where I had been for the missing time. I was too embarrassed to say, plus I wasn't keen on opening my mouth, so I did what I did best: I became as invisible as possible. I made friends with those who teased me the least about my teeth. I could easily deal with all the other insults and name-calling, but that one cut deeply. Despite my shortcomings and low self-esteem, some people initially liked me. I calculated that the new initial acceptance lasted, on average, three to six months. After that, there was always a form of rejection. A skill I picked up as a result was continually lowering my expectations of people. This way, I minimized the agony of rejection or disappointment. I was in control of how excluded I was. When I successfully reduced all expectations to zero, I could work on building myself up. I didn't realize how long first impressions lasted. People then naturally assumed I was now just being lucky to get things right because I was so successful at appearing worthless.

As a result, I would now start to find rejection in everything I did and said. I applied this to jobs that I signed up for and didn't get, phone numbers that girls wouldn't give me, promotions I didn't receive, phone calls that went unanswered, text messages not replied to, invitations to events that never came, and so on.

In relationships, too, I always anticipated rejection, and it always came. I wouldn't even try to fight it; to me, it was always inevitable. So, I gave my partners little effort, thinking they would leave anyway. Why invest so much energy and time in something that wouldn't last?

The Mother of all Rejection came when I had truly attached myself to someone in a relationship. This one hit hard. The relationship was falling apart, and like a load of sand dumped in a pit, I felt a pile of rejection dumped on me. I felt pointless, lifeless, and hopeless. I had begun to feel I had hit rock bottom and was waiting to bounce back up. While I languished, I started thinking about myself and my happiness for the 1st time I can remember. Did my happiness matter? Did I matter? If I just disappeared, would anyone even notice? I didn't want to fade from existence.

I was at an actual low point and began to shut down. I started shutting down my dreams, ambitions, hopes, joy, and heart. I was in survival mode. This is when I discovered the true power of words. There was one sentence that had a profound effect on me. It still has an impact today. Someone looked at me one day and declared, "You do not exist." In more ways than one, I almost ceased to exist. There was no getting any lower; I had hit the very bottom of the pit. I was barely able to function. I was just about managing to eat (although this became a task at one point), sleep, and go to and from work.

This is when I finally realized that because I was always on the lookout for rejection and focusing so much energy on thinking about it, I was rejecting myself and, by extension, God. I am His masterpiece; if I reject His work, I reject Him. I felt like I had been sleeping and suddenly woke up. After years of slumber, I started to enjoy life and being alive. I was determined to distance myself from the me, slowly dying of nothingness.

For the first time in forever, I began to live again, but just as I was beginning to feel that there was hope and a chance for happiness, I ruptured my Achilles tendon during a friendly game of squash. While recovering, I was immobile with an estimated three-month recovery time. Imagine getting a new lease on life and then having it away from me. It was more than I could bear, and so I slipped back into the pit of despair, loneliness, and rejection. I cried out to the Lord, but not for salvation. I didn't ask the Lord to rescue me; I asked Him to end it. I told Him I could not carry on and did not want to live any longer. Well, the Lord, God of His promises and mercies, showed me what it looked like to be granted my wish. "Ask and it shall be given..." Within four hours of making my plea, I was in the back of an ambulance on my way to A&E (Accident & Emergency) or Intensive care, suffering from PE (pulmonary embolism), a blood clot in the lungs.

While lying in the back of the ambulance, being blue-lighted to A&E, I rethought my original request and asked God if I could change my mind. Fortunately, God saw favor with me and granted my wish to stick around for a bit longer. This pit jam was the jolt I needed to shock life and purpose in me. Everything was now possible. I realized that life was too short to worry about the things I was magnifying. I was so grateful to God for giving me a second chance. My doctors must have thought I was a little crazy or just lacked understanding of my situation, as I was shockingly joyful.

I was in ICU for three days, where I was monitored constantly with several intravenous tubes attached to me. I was on a new type of blood-thinning drug. The doctors came around regularly with a somber look reserved for the more severe cases. They informed me of how serious the condition I was in and how lucky I was to be alive. They didn't understand why I was so happy and thought I did not understand how serious my predicament was.

On the contrary, I fully understood why I was so cheerful. I had never felt so alive in a long time. All my burdens and cares were gone! God has given me some more time. I didn't even know if I would make it out of the hospital, so I didn't want to waste any time wallowing in sorrow and ruminating on rejection. I smiled and joked and spoke to anyone who would listen to any subject that was of interest. I made friends with everyone in my ward: the other patients, the doctors, the nurses, the cleaners, the porters, and even visitors.

I was highest in my lowest. Fear began to lose its grip on me. I felt that God had a plan for me, and while working on His plan, I had nothing to fear. When I was discharged, I left the hospital a changed man. I no longer wore the garment of rejection. I agreed to help wherever I could for whoever asked. I agreed to assist the Pathfinders (a club for teens) in my church. I escorted a small UK contingent to Oshkosh (an international Pathfinders Camporee) in the US that year. It was a great experience, but the most epic part of the trip was the over 900-mile drive across four states on the wrong side of the road. We took our time to get there, but the journey back was a scene from "Rush Hour." The drive back had to be done in one day, as we had to catch our flights back to the UK. But like I said, I felt God had personally given me this mission, so I was never worried. I was entirely free from fear for the first time since childhood.

Exiting the pit, I finally accepted that I could achieve little by myself and handed everything to God. To be who God wanted me to be, I first learned to accept myself. When I started loving myself, others began reacting to me differently.

Since my exit from the pit, people have expressed that they like my poetry. My employer has said they appreciate me for my work ethic and experience. I have been told that I am a valued member of the church, a friend, and an accountability partner. None of this seemed possible from the pit's view.

Now, when rejection comes, instead of feeling rejected, I see it as a blessing because it means I am living, doing things, and learning. I also remember how many of the prophets and Jesus Himself were rejected, so I am in good company.

I have learned to accept who I am. My mistakes are evidence of my willingness to take risks; my faults set me apart. After all, how can I expect anyone else to like me if I don't like myself? I stopped trying to be like the person I never was and began being myself. Once I accepted myself, so did everyone else.

I was born for a great purpose. I now see my birth as the most incredible day of my life. I came here to be a blessing to others. I am no longer bound by rejection; by God's grace, I am a worthy cornerstone.

Meet Ted Reaves

Ted was born in the UK to Caribbean parents and resides in London. He is a devoted father to his beautiful daughter, who is the apple of his eyes.

Ted has been passionate about writing poetry and stories since he was very young. He shares his talents through spoken word and storytelling to encourage others in their faith and life journeys.

Ted Greaves is a computer security consultant who has worked in IT (information technology) for several years. He is always happy to help others with his expertise. He also extends his services in other areas, including volunteering with various organizations that work with young people to build their confidence and affirm their identity.

In 2009, Ted found a home in the SDA church, a place where his faith has continued to grow and shape his life. He is always eager to share his testimonies of God's intervention in his life at his local church.

As a long-standing member of several men's groups and ministries, Ted is dedicated to uniting men to make a positive difference in their families and communities. He is encouraging his brothers to be open, understanding, and accountable.

CHAPTER 12

Pain, Healing and Redemption: Jean's Journey of Faith

> *Let us therefore come boldly unto the throne of grace, that we may obtain mercy, and find grace to help in the time of need.* **(Hebrews 4:16)**

I have been hearing the following words resounding in my spirit lately: freedom, intelligence, joy, abundance, redeemed, liberty. These are some of the areas of deliverance God restored in me after enduring childhood trauma. God wanted me to live abundantly and free from judgment, suppression, and oppression.

My story is about my healing journey through forgiveness and how I found liberty, freedom, and redemption through Christ Jesus. It details how God had me waiting in a room of healing to furnish me for His service.

I was about six years old when someone first touched my body in a sexual manner. I was not aware of what was happening to me, so I just continued with my life. I didn't know what private parts entailed, who could touch or who wasn't allowed to touch me at that age. I was utterly clueless. But the body keeps the score, and I was traumatized but did not know it. The wound was kept latent for years until it manifested in different ways, especially when I became an adult.

Some of my trauma responses showed up through anxiety for no apparent reason. Some of it manifested through my childhood from age six straight up to age twenty-nine, where I had strong sexual urges. I couldn't explain any of it until God revealed to me that I had invisible wounds that I had for years that others couldn't see and I was unaware of. My younger sister and some family members often commented that they found me tense for reasons they could not fathom. I also took most things personally and would be easily offended by everything. I didn't realize that how I presented myself and responded to people was because I had been bleeding from an invisible wound for two decades.

I was in a pit of struggle, not knowing it or understanding its depth for years. As I grew older, I had forgotten that the unfavorable experiences at age six had even happened! Nobody knew what I had endured because I had buried it. After all, it is a difficult thing to share. I blamed myself for it as a child, so I didn't say anything.

There were comments made during my previous relationships that hurt and intensified my invisible wounds. Some other symptoms of my trauma included being attracted to the wrong people who were pursuing me for the wrong reasons. These are complicated emotions for a young girl to deal with, and I suffered with these circumstances for years. I had no one to talk to about it and no positive space to have these conversations in primary school. I later went to a boarding school, and this didn't help me mentally with the stress, but it was obviously good for me to gain the education I am grateful for.

Because I had a gaping wound, I ended up seeking love, attention, and comfort in the wrong places and ended up having a child at age 17 with someone who had no interest in keeping the pregnancy. He was also a teen and was petrified. This was another big wound and burden I had to carry on top of what I had already experienced. I would have kept hemorrhaging on others like the woman with the issue of blood recorded in Luke 8, but God saw my pain, heard my silent cry, and arranged for me to get on a journey of healing. At the point of writing this chapter, my daughter is 13 years old, and I am grateful that God had placed me on the healing journey so I can adequately parent a teenager and better understand how to handle her insecurities and know how to manage any signs of behavioral change she may display, due to my experience.

My healing journey started after leaving work one evening and walking through the mall window shopping. I suddenly saw a beautiful black lady with a hairstyle similar to mine. Immediately, I said hi and complimented her hair. Besides the hair, I was drawn to her and felt we had something in common. We kept in contact, and I found out she resided in the local area close to us. We made contact and then arranged to go to an art gallery show and volunteer at a shelter. Weeks later, we went ice skating and then to a museum. Our friendship grew from there, and I realized that this friendship was a blessing from God. He provides in our time of need.

After being friends for a while, we shared our struggles, and I was so grateful for this connection because I had not long come out of a relationship that did not work out and needed an outlet to air my pain. So, it was a timely divine connection that I had with this friend.

After a while, she told me about her bishop and his wife, who had the gift of prophecy. I requested a phone appointment to pray with him. When I got the chance to speak to him,

He started to prophesy in numbers of 6, and instantly, my eyes opened, and I was able to see, feel, and hear the 6-year-old in me who was abused. I felt sad and emotionally vulnerable for days. I had buried the situation deep for almost two decades of my life. Over that week, I cried and prayed ceaselessly and had a long cathartic conversation with God. It was also revealed that because of what happened over the years, I had attracted predatory men. I started reading books to help me process what childhood trauma and childhood molestation were.

During the process, I had troubling intrusive thoughts at times, asking myself, *Why me?* But in all this, the bottom line was that God had revealed all this through His Spirit. He didn't just evoke these dark memories for no reason. He had revealed this to bring me out of the misery that had been plaguing me subconsciously for years.

I started to heal in the following weeks. Week one was difficult because I had opened the wound afresh, but God sent his spirit to comfort me and help me endure the painful revelation. My prayers were contrite and intense. I listened to podcasts, and God took care of the rest.

I remember the bishop telling me to forgive people intentionally because it held me back. This wasn't easy, but I dove in. By doing this, I traded my sorrow in exchange for joy. Psalm 139:17-18 "How precious are your thoughts about me. When I wake up, you are still with me." This was one of the Scriptures that brightened my spirit and brought me peace.

During the process, I had a dream that took me back to the timeline of my first primary school, where I was being bullied. I felt this memory resurfaced to help me release the infection from my emotional wounds. It was in the early hours, around 3 am, mid-winter season in January 2024.

I was in a dream where I was taken back to my childhood playground in my first primary school in Kenya. In this dream, I started wondering why I was there. Spiritually, I couldn't connect the dots until three days later when I shared this experience with my Christian friend T. In sharing this story, the Holy Spirit revealed to us during a conversation why I was there.

I was brought back because I had to deal with the strongholds that shackled me from this time of my life when I was a child. Suddenly, I got a flashback to the classroom where I sat when I was about eight. I used to sit next to a mean boy called Joshua. He stole my pencils and threatened to stab my fingers with them if I told the teacher what he was doing. I felt intimidated and fearful of him. I was tiny, and he was a big boy. So, I felt defenseless, and I didn't want him to hurt me. He occasionally punched me if I tried to defend myself.

I also remembered how much I loved playtime, but I recall being weirdly approached by students of older age groups, some of whom were in their last year of school, asking me out even though I was only around eight years old. I didn't think much of it, but I knew this wasn't okay for my age. I didn't know the difference between which friends were innocent and which ones could take advantage of me. No one was there to talk to or give advice. So, I just left this topic unchecked. This may have opened a door for negative strongholds.

As we considered the dream and the memories resurfacing, T said, "Maybe it's because God wants you to heal from these experiences; He wants to heal your inner child from the stronghold of being defenseless. He wants to free you from the spirit of being harassed, trampled on, and bullied, so these strongholds don't go in the next chapter of your life and become generational." We then got on our knees and prayed using specific prayer points to break free from every stronghold of past childhood trauma and to declare what God says I am. With God, I am not defenseless. He is my refuge, my fortress, my Rock of Ages. I prayed specifically to be freed by the anointed blood of Jesus from the spirit of harassment, defenseless and predatory spirits. We do not fight against flesh and blood but against powers and principalities (Ephesians 6:12). Apostle Paul likened the ministry of God's servants to spiritual warfare. He said the weapons of our warfare are not carnal, but mighty through

God to the pulling down of strongholds (2 Corinthians 10:4). For we are overturning reasonings and every lofty thing raised against the knowledge of God. I prayed and thanked God for bringing things to the surface and revealing things to me. I prayed that He would complete the good work of healing me.

The thing with pain is you can't keep it in; you must let it out. Like a river, you've got to let it flow out of its source from inside so that you don't drown in it. It's like little streams flowing by the roadside after heavy rains. When they are flowing out into the drainage, they make lovely sounds. Sounds that are rhythmic and comforting. So, when the tears flow, let them fall so you can find relief. Psalm 144:15 states: "Happy are those people whose God is the future." While my river of pain flowed, God reached out his hand in the streams and caught me. He didn't let me drown.

After my horrible first week, the following weeks were filled with indescribable peace. I started thinking differently. I began to feel worthy. Yes, I went through a lot, but my God sees me as remarkable. I am his beloved daughter. His thoughts about me are precious. I stopped shaking or fidgeting when I spoke to my colleagues. Before my encounter with God, these were coping mechanisms that the body had adopted. Working with other people can be stressful and intimidating because of my low self-efficacy. So, each time my body was stressed, I swayed to calm it. I no longer rocked from carrying a two-decade burden on my body. I could stand solidly on the ground with my two feet anchored and be there in the present without fearing or feeling inadequate. I started carrying and presenting myself confidently. I was calm; I found peace.

Another thing that the Lord had healed me from is the pain of rejection, which was linked to people-pleasing and overcompensating so that I could feel accepted. The thing about rejection is that when it happens once or twice, you may be able to endure it, but when it occurs multiple times, each time, the wound deepens and leaves you feeling worthless. These then start to grow and lead to negative behavior and low self-perception, which leads to depression and anxiety. These wounds can only be restored by God because He sees everything that has happened to you. He knows every detail of your issue connected to your victory and breakthrough. That is why it is crucial to come back to God with all our broken pieces so that He can restore us. Since He is the One who manufactured all the different parts of us, it is best that He leads us through the processes of repair and maintenance, salvation and freedom, and righteousness.

Did you know that hating somebody is a habit parallel to loving someone? Once God started healing me, I started praying for those who hurt me and found it in my heart to love them. I started declaring abundance and fullness in their lives. I found that as my prayers went on, where there was heartache before, there was now a feeling of peace and compassion. It was like sorrow had transformed into joy.

I feel that God is calling me into ministry for healing in specific areas, including rejection and emotional or spiritual wounds for people. He is calling me to form a sisterhood of support for people who may have gone through similar experiences and different forms of pain and struggle. If you have been dealing with similar issues, I would encourage you to approach God's presence and be vulnerable with Him. Tell him how you feel. Tell him what upsets you and what hurts. He already knows, but your acknowledgment shows that you are willing and ready to take the journey of healing and change. Start addressing your pain. He is a good listener. You can journal difficult feelings and then begin to pray about them. Give it all to Him and stop nursing it with otherworldly things because the Creator knows the type of remedy that you need.

Make your prayers specific and say: *"Father, help me to forgive_____. It's difficult for me to forgive this person but help me find the strength and mercy to forgive them just like you forgave me. When I was at my worst, you still loved and forgave me. Help me find the grace to forgive others who have hurt me."* When you declare that you are healed, believe it and say, *"I will not be bound by sickness or trauma because, by Your stripes, I am healed. Your words are final in my life."* You are worth more than all the negative emotions that have plagued you. Your identity is not tied to your struggles. In God's eyes, you are royalty.

Once Christ comes into your heart you will have the mind of Christ. You will be free in your thinking. Let go of what society thinks about you and start thinking of what God thinks about you. Start affirming your mind with Scriptures. Do not be afraid, for God did not give you a spirit of fear but a spirit of love, sound mind, and self-control (2 Timothy 1:7). Learn to pray against fear and command it to go out of your atmosphere because that is not what God wants for you. He wants you to feel good about yourself, think positively, and use your mind for creativity and hard work that promotes well-being.

Every believer goes through challenges, but you have kingdom identity and kingdom authority, which we ought to key into when faced with challenges. So, let us approach the throne of grace with fullest confidence, that we may receive mercy for our failures and grace to help in the hour of need (Hebrews 4:16).

I thank God for taking the time and ordering my steps through the events that led to my healing journey. I didn't realize how much I needed it. I am grateful for the way He orchestrated my deliverance and took me out of my pit of trauma. I want to encourage other people who may have been through a similar situation that it's time to address your pain with the Lord. Clean the skeletons out of your closet and present them to the Lord so He can work on these dry bones and resurrect peace, joy, and favor in your life.

Meet Jean Obungu

Jean is originally from Kenya but resides in the United Kingdom. She has been involved in various projects, such as poetry groups, both as a poet writer and in reciting performances. She is involved in women's empowerment by supporting women enduring similar hardships to what she suffered. She participates in charity programs in Kenya and Uganda and works with young people in education. She holds a degree in public health and is interested in health promotion and well-being.

She was raised a Christian and has been reading the Bible at the podium since she was four years old. She encountered God at 17 and has since pursued salvation and a walk after God's heart as an in-depth believer.

Jean is a passionate writer with a blog called Tales of Jean, which involves writing and recording various accounts of how faith is applied in her life. Her story is evidence of her faith in God and how He redeemed her through various hardships.

CHAPTER 13

From Dreaming to Trusting: A Journey of Faith and Writing

---- 66 ----

For I know the plans I have for you,'
declares the Lord, 'plans to prosper you and
not to harm you, plans to give you hope and
a future. (Jeremiah 29:11)

---- 99 ----

Born amidst the vibrant colors Jamaica and it's enchanting landscapes, my journey began with dreams as colorful and rich as the land that nurtured me. My name is Angela James, and from a young age, I harbored a burning desire to become a successful, award-winning author. Raised in a community where storytelling was woven into the fabric of everyday life, I was captivated by the power of words to transport and transform.

As a child, I would lose myself in the pages of books, devouring stories that ignited my imagination and fueled my aspirations. The lush Jamaican scenery provided the perfect backdrop for my creative endeavors, inspiring poetry that echoed the rhythm of the island and short stories that danced with the spirit of its people.

Growing up in Jamaica, I was surrounded by a rich tapestry of culture and creativity that served as the foundation for my aspirations as a writer. Among the towering figures that left an indelible mark on my impressionable mind were Jamaican icons like Oliver Samuel and Miss Lou. Their mastery of storytelling and performance captivated audiences near and far, instilling in me a deep-seated admiration for the power of words to entertain, enlighten, and inspire.

With his wit and humor, Oliver Samuel brought laughter to countless households across the island, his characters springing to life with each animated gesture and infectious laugh. Miss Lou, on the other hand, enchanted listeners with her soulful renditions of Jamaican folk tales and songs, preserving and celebrating the rich heritage of our people.

As I watched in awe, their performances solidified in me the possibility of budding and blooming into a prolific published author. If they could weave such magic with their words, then surely, I, too, could aspire to create worlds that would captivate the imagination and touch the hearts of readers far and wide.

As the island of Jamaica fed my imagination with its radiant colors and enrapturing landscapes, I found solace in creating worlds of my own within the confines of my mind. Even amid trying times, when life seemed filled with more shadows than sunlight, I would retreat into the sanctuary of my imagination, where anything was possible.

Neglected and forgotten, I clung to the visual imagery of beautiful stories that danced across the canvas of my mind, each one a beacon of hope amidst the darkness. In those moments, I discovered that the power of storytelling extended far beyond the pages of a book; it was a lifeline, a means of escape from the harsh realities of life.

With each word penned and each character brought to life, I felt myself blossoming and blooming like the flowers that dotted the Jamaican landscape. Though my circumstances may have been bleak, my imagination remained untamed and free, soaring to new heights with each story I crafted.

In the face of adversity, I drew strength from the resilience of my Jamaican roots, channeling the spirit of perseverance that coursed through the veins of my ancestors. They, too, had faced their share of trials and tribulations, yet they had emerged victorious, their indomitable spirit serving as a beacon of hope for future generations.

As I continued to nurture my love for storytelling, I faced the agony of defeat to have an audience or any validation through family support and publications. I was clueless about the prospect of publishing books. As a matter of fact, the stories that I dreamed up or jotted down were a way of escaping from the abusive and traumatic life I lived as a child. At times, it seems that the pain of life pushed me further and further into these fictional worlds, as life with neglect, abandonment, and abuse was all I saw and experienced. I began to believe that writing was not a fantasy and that my dreams would be cataloged as sheer illusions and fiction that would never come to pass.

Like Joseph, who dreamt of ruling over his family, I harbored dreams of becoming a successful author. Yet, within me, harsh criticism echoed, drowning out the voice of ambition. Doubts whispered, declaring I would never achieve literary greatness. With no visible signs of success, I concealed my aspirations, silent and hidden. I retreated from familial expectations, seeking solace in the sanctuary of my imagination.

In Genesis 37, Joseph's dreams foretold his ascendancy over his brothers despite their initial scorn. Similarly, my dreams faced skepticism and ridicule, leaving me to nurture them in solitude. Yet, like Joseph, I found refuge in my dreams. In the wilderness of doubt, I crafted stories where I found my own version of happily ever after. Just as Joseph's dreams ultimately came to fruition, I held onto the hope that my stories would someday find their place in the world, despite the doubts that plagued me.

Through the trials and tribulations, I drew strength from the resilience of biblical figures like Joseph, who persevered in the face of adversity. In the depths of my imagination, I continued to dream, knowing that even the most unlikely dreams can become reality with unwavering faith and determination.

My journey took a pivotal turn when I arrived in Canada, a land of opportunity, with my dreams clenched tightly in my heart. As I stepped onto the unfamiliar soil, hope surged, driving me forward despite the uncertainty looming ahead. Eager to pursue my passion for writing, I embarked on a quest to share my voice with the world.

I submitted my work of poetry to countless outlets, pouring my soul onto the pages, hoping to see my words in print and have my voice heard across continents. With each submission, I braced myself as I was prepared for the possibility of rejection, knowing that the path to success was often fraught with obstacles. Yet, nothing could prepare me for the relentless onslaught of disappointment that followed.

There was no warm embrace of acceptance. Instead, I was greeted with the cold sting of rejection. Each rejection letter felt like a blow to my spirit, threatening to extinguish the flames of my passion. Doubt crept in, gnawing away at my confidence, whispering tauntingly that perhaps my dreams were nothing more than foolish fantasies.

In those dark moments of despair, I questioned everything—my talent, worth, and purpose. I wondered if I had made a mistake in pursuing my dreams, if I was destined to forever remain on the sidelines, watching others bask in the spotlight of success. The weight of uncertainty pressed on me, suffocating my hopes and aspirations.

Yet, even in the depths of my despair, a flicker of determination refused to be snuffed out. With each rejection, I resolved to try again, to push forward despite the odds stacked against me. I sought solace in the words of encouragement from friends and loved ones, who reminded me that greatness often arose from the ashes of failure.

Drawing inspiration from the resilience of those who came before me, I refused to let the setbacks define me. I returned to the stories of biblical figures like Joseph, who persevered in the pit he was thrust into and the prison that held him captive, trusting in a higher purpose that transcended the trials of the present moment. I would make it to the palace one day.

As I continued to hone my craft, I found refuge and solace in the rhythm of pen against paper, the melody of words weaving together to form stories that reflected the depths of my soul. With each new creation, I discovered a sense of purpose that went beyond mere publication or acclaim—a profound connection to the world around me, a testament to the power of storytelling to bridge the divides that separate us. I began to write for myself.

I refused to let my dreams wither and die. With determination as my compass, I took matters into my own hands. I painstakingly crafted my first poetry book by hand, pouring my soul into every word, every page. I sold copies to friends and relatives, sowing the seeds of my dreams one book at a time.

Yet, just as the first buds of success bloomed, I faced a new trial. I found myself at the crossroads of motherhood and homelessness, my children's needs overshadowing my aspirations. With a heavy heart, I set aside my dreams, tucking them away in the recesses of my mind, where they lay dormant, waiting for the right moment to awaken once more.

Years passed, and I found myself in a new land, the United States of America, which had endless possibilities and second chances. It was here that the embers of my dreams were reignited, this time through the avenue of self-publishing.

With renewed fervor, I poured myself into my writing once more, hoping that this time, my efforts would bear fruit.

Slowly but surely, my perseverance began to produce results with every author's copy I bought. I started to create a library of my work as a reminder of who I am as a writer. Seeing my books on the shelves in my home were my faith becoming works, and they kept the flames of hope alive. I sold a few copies here and there, and the royalties gave me reasons to keep my faith that my breakthrough would happen one day.

Psalm 37:5: "Commit your way to the Lord; trust in Him, and He will do this: He will make your righteous reward shine like the dawn, your vindication like the noonday sun."

But as the years passed, I faced yet another obstacle. Despite my best efforts, the extent of my dreams and hopes seemed to elude my grasp. Rejection letters piled up, each one a testament to the uphill battle I face as a writer. Doubt crept in, whispering insidious lies of inadequacy and failure.

Proverbs 16:9: "In their hearts humans plan their course, but the Lord establishes their steps."

Faced with seemingly insurmountable odds, I questioned whether my path lay elsewhere. I turned to God and His word for guidance, seeking clarity amidst the chaos of uncertainty.

I often grappled with the possibility that perhaps my dreams were not in alignment with God's plan for my life, that my pursuits were fleeting desires in the grand tapestry of His divine will.

Isaiah 55:8-9 -" 'For my thoughts are not your thoughts, neither are your ways my ways,' declares the Lord. 'As the heavens are higher than the earth, so are My ways higher than your ways and My thoughts than your thoughts.'"

Through the highs and lows of my journey, I am learning that my validation as a prolific writer should not be based on sales or notoriety but from God. This means that God's plan is ideal for me, and I seek His validation and approval that I am living a life that is pleasing to Him. Jeremiah29:11 posits,"' For I know the plans I have for you,' declares the Lord, 'plans to prosper you and not to harm you, plans to give you hope and a future.'"

Each day, I wrestle with the tension between my desires and God's will. I look for solace in the knowledge that God's plans for me are far greater than anything I could imagine, even if it means letting go of the dreams I had held dear for so long. I cling to the belief that God's love, mercy, and grace will sustain me, even in the face of uncertainty and disappointment.

As I embrace the uncertainty of my future, I am gradually finding peace in surrendering my dreams to the hands of a loving God. I realize that true success lies not in the pursuit of my own ambitions but in trusting that God's plan for my life is perfect and complete. With each step forward, I am drawing strength from the knowledge that God's love will guide me through the wilderness of doubt and fear, leading me to a future filled with hope and promise.

Philippians 4:6-7 states, "Do not be anxious about anything, but in every situation, by prayer and petition, with thanksgiving, present your requests to God. And the peace of God, which transcends all understanding, will guard your hearts and your minds in Christ Jesus."

I write this chapter while I wait in my pit stop. I am allowing God to furnish me for His good work. As declared in Jeremiah 29:11, He knows His plans for me and that they are perfect. God is the author of my life; His accolades are grander than the most titled and decorated author. Hence, I trust Him to use me in whatever capacity He sees fit. I submit my will and desires to Him, and as He has given me this gift, I pray that He uses it for His honor and glory.

As my journey continues, I trust that it will be a testament to the transformative power of faith and trust in God's plan. Though the road may be fraught with challenges and uncertainty, I walk forward with confidence, knowing that my future is secure in the hands of a loving and faithful God. And even if my dreams of becoming a successful, award-winning author never come to fruition, I take comfort in the knowledge that God's plans for my life are far greater than anything I could ever imagine.

I find comfort in Psalm 37:4, "Delight yourself in the Lord, and He will give you the desires of your heart," and Proverbs 3:5-6 "Trust in the Lord with all your heart and lean not on your own understanding; in all your ways submit to Him, and He will make your paths straight."

Meet Angela James

As a dedicated educator with a fervent passion for the written word, Angela James has embarked on a transformative journey toward authorship. Inspired by biblical teachings and texts, she has woven profound messages into an eclectic array of genres, navigating the depths of the literary world while "Waiting in the Pit" for her moment to shine as a prolific writer.

Drawing upon years of experience in the classroom and possessing a deep well of inspiration, her work reflects a commitment to storytelling that enlightens, challenges, and uplifts. She strives to echo timeless truths with each page and share the wisdom gained from life's trials and triumphs.

CHAPTER 14

"Do, Lord, Remember Me."

The Lord hath appeared of old unto me, saying, Yea, I have loved thee with an everlasting love: therefore with lovingkindness have I drawn thee.
(Jeremiah 31:3)

"I was forced to do it!"
"My situation was not ideal."
"Did you not see that I was pushed into it?"
"If only I had some support or parameters."

I often found desperate reasons to justify my choices, thinking it was everyone's fault but mine. I did not realize that even though my situation impacted my behavior, I had a choice in the matter.

As a child, hearing the story of Adam and Eve, I could not fathom how Adam allowed Eve to convince him to eat the fruit. How and why did Eve do it? They had everything. Their lives were perfect. I knew exactly how the script should have gone, like watching a movie. They should not have eaten the fruit. It was so easy to conclude that looking in from the outside, I was about to have a rude awakening.

Like most children in Jamaica, I was a little girl raised affectionately in the Christian community. My mother and father were married, and I lived with them and six siblings. The eldest sibling had already moved out by the time I was born. My parents' marriage was different from your typical role-model-award-winning marriage. Even at a very young age, I knew it was a rollercoaster ride with steep, sustained drops. It was not an amusement park, and I didn't get the option to hop on. I was in it and strapped in tightly. The ebb and flow of shouting, quarrels, and fights had created anxiety, frustration, and fear for me and all my siblings. We were all on the ride; we were children who needed to be where our parents were.

Despite the chaos that sometimes happened in my home while growing up, there were extraordinary days when bonding with siblings, mother, and father was blissful. One of my favorite times with my dad was listening to or watching cricket. We would wake each other up when the game was going to be played in a country that had a different time zone, sometimes in the dead of the night or early morning hours. In our own little way, that created a unique bond and communication among us.

My mother stayed home and took care of us. I enjoyed her cooking and teachings on how to be a child of God. While my mother was good at her vocation, one thing that I found astonishing growing up was her blind faith.

We did not have everything I wanted growing up. Sometimes, we did not even have those things that we needed. But we had a comfortable home, unlike many, as my parents had purchased their home and had to maintain a mortgage along with seven children. You can imagine how hard that was. We mostly had our necessities, maybe not the finest clothes or the fanciest furniture, but we were managing, considering the situation.

During the times when school fees were due and we were short on food, my mother would unapologetically tell us that God would work it out. I remember when my sister's teacher's college tuition needed to be paid, and there was zero dollars. My mother calmly said, "God is going to work it out." She got dressed and told us she would be right back. When she returned, she presented the evidence of her faith. Somehow, God provided the money through a person who could help her. The faith she had and the answers I saw convinced me that God is real.

The testimonies witnessed and shared solidified that faith. My sister shared that when they had nothing to eat, my mother made dinner that evening without knowing where the food would come from. They sang songs of praise, and not long after, there was a knock on the door, and food went like a room service delivery! These miracles always blew my mind and secured my belief and love for God.

By age eleven, my older siblings left home one by one. Two of us were left at home: my younger brother and me. From my perspective at the time, my siblings got out! But who was coming for the rest of us? Now, the inevitable had finally happened. We were still on that mental roller coaster, but my mom tapped out and drifted further from my dad. As she drifted, she carried my brother and me to another church, away from the one we all attended, leaving my dad alone to worship there. She was convicted that the Seventh Day Adventist Church was where God was calling her.

I was about ten years old when we started attending the Seventh-day Adventist church, and my brother was nine. In about a year, I got baptized with my brother in the "We Shall Behold Him Crusade, 2000." I was so happy to walk with Jesus, and I was getting involved in the Pathfinder, the children's choir, and the mass choir. I had a church friend, Rose, with whom I would go to lunch at her home for a few

Sabbaths, after which we would go to AY (youth worship service).

It was good to have other children around me and learn that God loves me. You see, growing up, I was never the favorite in any capacity. I was always the outcast, the one taken for granted, the bullied, the less fortunate. I often wonder why people were so cruel; why couldn't people love people? Why would they want to hurt someone? However, it got better when I became a senior in high school.

Because of this initial unkind attitude people had towards me, I took comfort and found a friend in Jesus, who proved repeatedly that He loved me. I would always talk to Him, as He was my genuine friend on whom I could always depend.

In retrospect, it was not all bad regarding having friends. Despite the unkind treatment from many, I had a great childhood interacting with the other children in my neighborhood.

As I got older, I better understood Adam and Eve's story. My brother and I were left alone like Eve to decide who we would serve. We were cleft in the dip of the roller coaster as my mother had jumped off and left us with our father, who was going to a different church. My brother and I went to church for a few Sabbaths, but gradually, that changed. We started going outside to play in the afternoon and soon in the morning. We always felt guilty each step we took over the line. But it had gotten so easy that I did not even consider the Sabbath sacred. I would go to the supermarket, the shops, and events easily. This was the beginning of sorrow. I was lost, and I numbed myself to that fact. I did not want to feel the ultimate betrayal. I did not want to face how I was turning my back on God.

Three years later, I found myself going to parties in high school. I was going to lab classes and games on Sabbaths. During these times of drifting further and further, my mind was being permeated with a beam of light through a story my mom and siblings often spoke about. I always thought it was a ridiculous story. It was not possible.

My sister, Liz, was jokingly called a "reader woman" (a fortune teller). You see, she had a dream about our family when she was a small child. She dreamt that most of us would all leave the church. My mother shared that Liz and Karen were going to baptize first, and then they would later leave the church when they became adults, but they would return. Andre, my big brother, would own a business. Gene, my bigger sister, would not go into the church initially or get baptized with us, and my brother Pete would become a pastor.

I was shocked as I contemplated the dream because most of it had materialized. My bigger sister was not in the church; my sisters had come out of the church, my brother owned his own business, and my brother started preaching and holding Bible studies, though he was not yet a pastor. Before that, my mother, when she was pregnant with Pete, also had a dream that her children would leave the church, but they would return. Why was I reflecting on these dreams? I was not even born when they had them. Yet, during my despair, when I was stuck and languishing in the prison of my mind, all I could think of was that God said my mother's children would return to the fold. I held on to that promise for dear life. That beam of light stood in the back of my head even as I was held captive by the devil.

My high school graduation was approaching, and I was having a great time with my friends. High school was not easy in my junior years; however, I loved the end. I was bonding with a small group of good girls and thought life was good. By now, my moral compass had degraded. It had shifted to me feeling unworthy of God's love. However, growing up hanging with mostly boys taught me many things. I was practicing numbing in this instance. I had perfected it, so I did what I did, almost as if I was unaware of my surroundings. I was doing so many things that were unbecoming of my Christian conviction, and I was convinced that God could not love me anymore. I could not go back to Him. I was predestined; *I wouldn't make it*, I thought. These thoughts I had created the perfect springboard for what I thought was the best-laid plan of the enemy.

One evening, my friends were talking about sins and their weight. One friend, Leslie, who I respected as she and her mother were Christians, weighed in on the matter, "My mom said that sin is sin; if you are sinning in one way, it's all the same, might as well do all." I felt a feeling of guilt, shame, and great disappointment. The thought crowded my mind again that God couldn't love me because I had turned my back on Him, and what's done is done. I might as well live my life in sin.

A part of me felt liberated! As I clicked play and rewind what my friend told me, I thought about my first boyfriend. I had told him that I would not have sex before I got married. I desperately wanted to hold on to that part that gave me a lifeline to God. But now, it didn't matter! I was already sinning. As Leslie outlined, what was it to add one more? After all, they are all the same. My boyfriend was ecstatic! A few days later, I jumped over that bridge. Going over that bridge soon led me to the highway, with broad roads and many lanes, leading to my destruction.

I went to college after high school, and this is where I maxed out. I went from only going to one or two parties to multiple parties in one night. I had made connections with a friend, and we went from parties to bars to clubs and strip clubs. I was drinking more than I ever did, and more often, I was looking for the next high, the next excitement. I was trying to silence the voice of the Holy Spirit. I wanted to go further and further, not to remember my betrayal of God. In the noise and the chaos in my head, I could only remember a piece of a song that I knew. "Do Lord remember me." That was my prayer throughout my years of defiance.

The distractions of parties, clubs, and drinking were great fillers. Even after leaving school and starting work, I did not give up the opportunity to attend different events. However, after a season, things began to change. Those opportunities died down, leaving me with an overwhelming sadness. I was home and not working then, so you can imagine the overwhelming thoughts that intruded. At one point, I felt like my brain was short-circuiting. I needed someone to call! I needed an event, an outing. I was desperate to fill the void.

Finally! My guy friends called me up to hang out! The drought was over, and I got picked up. A female friend and two of my male friends came to get me. The music was nice, and they had my favorite, apple vodka! We chatted as the music played, and I took a sip of magic. I had not drunk in a little bit during my entertainment drought. As I eagerly brought the cup to my mouth and took a sip, I got the shock of my life! It was repulsive and had the most unpleasant taste. Yet, everyone else seemed to be okay. I carried on through the night, ate, and had "a time," but I was unsure if it was a good time. I was in a daze and bewildered by my drink and my interests. I did not think about it at that moment, but I knew something supernatural was happening to me. I could only pray, "Do, Lord, remember me."

For several months, my interest in hanging out was less intense. I was most disappointed with myself after a two-month relationship ended. It was my second relationship, and I felt downhearted, but in a different way. I could now feel the void, but I knew it would not be filled with the next big entertainment. I still prayed, "Do, Lord, remember me?"

In December 2012, during my lay low period, my childhood friend, brother, and I sat in front of my house, just chatting as we often do. Something interesting happened that Friday. My friend, who was not a Christian and knew I grew up being one, said, "Sheridan, (it's a) long time since you have not gone to church; let us go tomorrow." With great shock and relief, I eagerly agreed as if waiting for someone to invite me. I went to church intending to return to God, only to turn back as I stepped into the churchyard. I could not face that trial. I could not forgive myself for what I had done. God could not love me after everything. I was a little scared but happy that at least I had a friend to go with who was not "holy," so to speak.

That night, I went into my room and decided to study my quarterly (Sabbath School Lesson Study) as I would do years gone when I went to church. I have no memory of what that lesson entailed, but I knew that it grabbed my attention. I lived in the song "As the deer panteth for the water, so my soul longeth after Thee." I watched a sermon that spoke about giving my life to God. As I listened, I recommitted my life to God! I took His hand as He extended it and lifted me from the life of wreckage on the roller coaster, perpetually holding me in sin.

The next Sabbath morning, I went to church with my childhood friend. It was different than the other times I had gone. I was determined to go to the altar. As the altar call was made, I eagerly signed the card.

As I was lifted from the rollercoaster, my thoughts became confused. How could Jesus come for me in the pit of wreckage after all I had done? Though Jesus was carrying me, I had this heavy feeling in my heart. I mentally could not grasp this unmerited favor. I did not deserve it! I hated myself more.

A couple Sabbaths passed, and I brought my nieces and nephews along with my sisters who had not gone to church for years. It was such a miracle knowing that I heard God's call and was responding to it, and now inspired my sisters to join me but I was still in turmoil. My baptism date was set by a Bible worker who reached out to me during the week.

The following week came, and my Bible mentor called me that Friday evening. She confirmed that the time had come and wanted to walk me through the details of the baptism. I shared with her that I was not going to baptize that Sabbath.

The Sabbath morning, after telling her I would not join, I showed up to church with my sisters, two nephews, and two nieces. We were all dressed and ready to go in and have a beautiful Sabbath.

While we stood in the parking lot that morning, I looked at my family as we walked in. As if I was arrested by a thought and a force I could not resist, I told them, "I am not staying here; I will be going to Portmore Seventh Day Adventist Church." You can imagine my sisters' perplexity as they pondered why I would leave one church where I had a ride and go to a different church. My sister Liz was the sternest, thinking that this was foolishness.

I did not know what to feel as I walked out of the churchyard. I was leaving the church where I had spent the latter part of my childhood years to attend a church I had only visited once. I could not understand it; however, it felt like I was prompted by something beyond me. I got a taxi quickly and was on my way to church.

I walked into the Portmore SDA church to a youthful program. As I perused the room, I could tell it was a special day. My eyes were captivated by the sign that ran across the curtains on the backdrop, "My Lover, My Jesus, My Friend." I felt butterflies and a sense of joy in my stomach. It was as if I was being medicated from my illness of unforgiveness and not surrendering. Jesus had taken me out of Satan's roller coaster and placed me on the ground, but I was still wobbling. I was dizzy with the lies being fed to me by the enemy. Unforgiveness was seeping through my veins as I could not forgive myself for what I had done to my God, even though He was clasping me in His arms. As if the butterflies were not enough, their theme song melted my heart.

"Falling in love with Jesus, falling in love with Jesus, falling in love, with Jesus, was the best thing I've ever done. In His arms, I feel protected, in His arms never disconnected. There's no place I'd rather be..."

Everything now made sense. God wanted me here. He knew what I needed to hear. It was a perfect play of God's word in Jeremiah 31:3. The sermon was excellent! I could hear the pastor lovingly pouring out his heart, saying, "Jesus loves you! He loves you!"

I had been accused for so long by the enemy. I had done so much. The list of all my sins was long. I had now come to contend with them all within this service, at this church that the Holy Spirit had drawn me to. Like Adam and Eve in the Garden of Eden, I had hidden long enough, played the blame game, and made excuses. I thank God that when I chose to surrender, He stretched out His hands, and through the pastor's voice, He told me, "I love you; I gave my life to save you." At that moment, my burden was released.

The event at the church was a youth revival, and though I had gotten my answer, it was further solidified as I went to the services nightly. I walked up to God most nights to the altar crying. I needed this release. It felt like I was in therapy.

Finally, the Sabbath came again, and I was a part of that number to be baptized. I happily, without hesitation, publicly displayed my commitment and love to my God in the beautiful marriage of baptism, and I have not turned back since.

There Have been hills and valleys on my Christian journey, but I am no longer trapped in the pit of a roller coaster. God answered my prayer. He remembered me! Oh, what love!

Meet Sherian Jordon

An ardent lover of her Heavenly Father and the quintessential family and friendship person who values relationships and quality time over any material acquisitions is the best way to describe Sherian Christal Jordon.

Sherian, the "Songbird" as she is affectionately called, was born in Kingston, Jamaica. She currently lives with her husband, Kevin Jordon, in South Florida, U.S.A. She believes there is no opportunity for ministry, too little or too great, for her to accomplish for Christ once He calls her to do it. She is from a large, close-knit family, which has helped shape her into who she is today. Without much forethought, she goes above and beyond for others, not just because of her conviction that the Lord has called us to be gracious, loving, and kind, but because that's just who she is and how she was raised.

Sherian has a true passion for youth outreach. When she is not belting out notes in worship or ministry to others, she is persistently and lovingly empowering the young people both in and outside her family. She encourages them to be their best selves spiritually and socially, with the Bible as her unwavering reference. She believes it is the indisputable measuring stick through which we gauge our thoughts, actions, and words, a testament to the strength of her faith.

CHAPTER 15

Rescued from the Pit of Doubt

Therefore if any man be in Christ, he is a new creature: old things are passed away; behold, all things are become new. (2 Corinthians 5:17)

C hristianity was something that I mocked and scoffed at since I was eleven. It was a lifestyle that I did not want to associate with due to my Rastafarian father's influence and the poor representation of Christian principles displayed by family members who were professed Christians. Their behavior left much to be desired; hence, I was never attracted or felt compelled to join the throng of "hypocrites." It got to the point where I used to blaze and jeer my two siblings, who were churchgoers, hollering, "Christophine and Seven Devil," whenever I saw them dressed for church.

Despite my actions and words, I always knew there was a God. During my upbringing, there were moments when my grandmother taught me the word of God, and I was convicted of God's existence but was never impressed to worship Him in a formal setting.

As a young man, my main priority was football. I loved this sport from a tender age, and it became my everything. I dreamed of becoming the "creme de la crème" of football/soccer. For this reason, I slept with the ball as a little boy and sometimes pretended that I was sick so that I could train and practice my skills at home during school hours. Thus, since I was exceptionally good at playing the sport, I traveled several times to represent my country abroad. Unfortunately, my academic achievements were sacrificed as all my time and effort was invested in my cherished sport.

I lived with my aunt (my father's sister) at age fourteen. This is where I was properly introduced to Christianity, where I embraced it, and where a lot of changes were made in my life. Due to the principles and positive environment in the home, such as Sabbath preparation, exposure to the Bible, and encouragement from my aunt and her husband, it came to the point where I discontinued uttering all obscene language and desisted from drinking alcoholic beverages. But there was room for improvement. I was still a womanizer and a Sabbath-breaker.

After failing my studies because of being engrossed in football, I got to Form 3 with a conditional pass. Thus, I had to do much better academically in that form to be promoted to Form 4. I applied myself to my lesson, and by God's grace, I did much better and was promoted to Form 4. This was when I experienced the turning point in my life, both educationally and spiritually. I became a class monitor for the first time and was selected to serve as a prefect in Form 5. In addition, I made a major decision and took the bold step towards baptism.

A televised crusade intrigued me, and when I finished playing soccer in the evenings, I would tune into the channel. I was astonished and impressed with what I was hearing from the preacher. Pastor Claudius Morgan, a world-renowned evangelist who has brought many souls to Jesus through his ministry, was the evangelist for this campaign. On the final night of the crusade, my aunt invited me to accompany her, and I went. When I got there, everyone was garbed in white outfits except me. I was dressed in black and white. It was the candle ceremony night.

At the beginning of the message, the preacher said, "One thing we are going to have tonight is baptism." I was so traumatized because the reason I accepted the invitation to go on the final night was because I thought there would have been no baptism. Though troubled, I stayed until the end of the message, when they turned off the lights so the candlelights could shine. The view was spectacular and appealing. While the candle lights shone, the preacher began to make the altar call. An usher was standing beside me, urging me to get baptized. She beckoned to me twice. I then reflected on my life. I said to myself, "Lord, is this Your glory? If so, I want to be a part of it." I was in awe. I took a moment, did some self-introspection about my life, and considered several things.

I first thought about my health. When my father passed away, I had severe chest pains that almost resulted in a heart attack. I could not sleep with the lights off because I had this theory that my father would come back and hammer me with licks. Therefore, I was afraid to sleep in the dark, and that triggered a lot of chest pain. I thought about football. There was a point in my football career where my performance was not consistent, and because of this, I had a bitter experience with the fans. So, I told myself, Lord, I will play better if I give you my life.

I thought of my ex-partner. She was my first love, but I did not treat her as she deserved. I would boldly disrespect her and entertain other women. Consequently, both of us decided to end the relationship. She, however, started a relationship with someone else. It was excruciating seeing her with another person because I still loved her. Therefore, I wanted to get baptized so she could see the change in me and we could get back together.

I also thought about my father and his life choices. I didn't want to depart this life without knowing Jesus. Thus, I didn't want to take the path of my father. My father had some loving sides to him, but he had some unbearable faulty characteristics.

Therefore, with all those considerations, I said, "I am going to grab this opportunity and give my life to Jesus." Then I turned to the usher beside me and told her, "I will give my heart to Jesus." As I was making my way for baptism, there was a wall along the way. This strange voice whispered, "Throw yourself over the wall." That night, the devil wanted to stop me from getting baptized. Nevertheless, I pressed through the dark and gave my heart to Christ. I believed that was the reason I was dressed in black and white. It was really for baptism. After all, black and white symbolizes death. And that night, I was buried and brought alive again. Praise God! My family and friends were shocked when they saw that I was baptized. When I got home, my cousin said to me, "Kimron, do you know what you did?" I told him, "Yes, I know what I did."

Everything about my life didn't change immediately, but I was conscious about my choice to follow Christ. One of my main challenges was playing football on the Sabbath. One

Sabbath, after participating in the communion service, I went home and saw my school football team playing at the park. The park is just a short distance from where I live, and I could not resist the temptation; I went and played. After the match, someone asked me, "Kimron, isn't today your Sabbath?" I was so ashamed.

When I got home, my aunt was enraged by what I had done. She said, "Kimron, you know today is the Sabbath, and you went to play football?" I was broken and distraught. I said, "God, I will take you seriously." That was the turning point because I took the Lord seriously from thereon, and God did the same. One afternoon, when I was communing with Him, I came across one of the most powerful verses of Scripture, John 14:15, which said, "If you love me, keep my commandment." When I came across that verse, I had a choice: either to break one of God's commandments by playing football on the Sabbath or to reverence God's holy day and give credence to it as I did the other nine. My mind was then pointed to the cross, where I reflected on that amazing sacrifice that Jesus made for me. I knelt, cried, and bellowed, "Lord, I love you a lot more than football." After this deep conviction that the Lord gave to me through His word, I never again went to play football on the Sabbath. Therefore, the Lord gave me victory. Praise God! Every Sabbath, I found myself in the house of God.

It got even sweeter. The Spirit of the Lord then drove me to read and study Scripture. I was amazed by the things God was revealing to me. Thus, as He revealed, I began to note what He told me in His words. The word of God cannot lie. "O taste and see that the LORD is good: blessed is the man that trusteth in him" (Psalms 34:8).

Indeed, I tasted Him, and He's truly good. Moreover, He healed me from my brokenness and from the hurts that I considered before I got baptized. He restored my health, healed my broken heart concerning my ex-partner, allowed me to release my unhealthy obsession with football, and gave me the peace and assurance that I did not have to walk the path of my father. I saw in the Lord greater things than I can ever imagine. He gave me new desires, different thoughts, and emotions. "Therefore, if any man be in Christ, he is a new creature: old things are passed away; behold, all things are become new" (2 Corinthians 5:17).

I got more good news. Because of my transformation, I was promoted to Form 5. In this form, I was a new Kimron. Therefore, all the light God revealed to me after I got baptized manifested itself in Form 5. My mantra became: "Let your light so shine before men, that they may see your good works, and glorify your Father which is in heaven" (Matthew 5:16).

"For I am not ashamed of the gospel of Christ: for it is the power of God unto salvation to everyone that believeth; to the Jew first, and also to the Greek" (Romans 1:16) Almost every lunch time, I gathered some students and invited them to do devotion with me. Everything that the Lord was showing me through His word, I was revealing to them. I was eager to do this. As time went by, more students started to attend the sessions. They had an urge to learn new things. Thus, the staff was delighted with what they saw and heard.

The time came when the prefects had to serve. Within the prefect body were head boys, head girls, deputy head boys, and deputy head girls. In retrospect, I can firmly say that one of the biggest successes where I have seen the goodness of God, His transforming power, and how He has been guiding me to accomplish things that I never thought possible was my appointment as the head boy of the Bethel High School in my country.

Additionally, I was doing exceptionally well at church: preaching, witnessing, and giving Bible study until I was attacked by the enemy spiritually. It was a massive blow. At that time, I was staying at my grandmother's house, where I grew up. She was getting older, and she wanted someone to stay with her. It was not easy at all. I had to deal with her as well as with my uncle, who has mental challenges while completing my School-based Assessments (SBAs) and participating in church activities. It was a heavy load to carry at that age. Therefore, Satan capitalized on my vulnerabilities. He attacked me when I was weak physically, mentally, and spiritually.

One day, I was by my eldest sister's residence, and her partner showed me a clip with this Jamaican guy stating that he did not believe in God or the Bible. I asked, "What am I hearing here?" I was distraught. It was the first time I heard someone say there was no God. However, I debated it with my sister's partner, but inside, I was troubled. When I went to pray that night, I could not. I was puzzled by the thoughts that lingered in my mind. Does God exist or not? Picture hearing something puzzling and trying to make sense of it for the first time. I found it difficult to shake my thoughts, but as time passed, I began to feel much better.

Then came another attack. "Be sober, be vigilant; because your adversary the devil, as a roaring lion, walketh about, seeking whom he may devour:" (1 Peter 5:8). One evening, my church was in the community witnessing, and at the end of it, a man came up to my friend saying, he did not believe in the Bible nor God. I debated again, but what he said left an impression on me. From there, I started struggling with praying once more. As a result of this, I discovered my weakness. Like Thomas, I was doubtful. The enemy planted a seed, and it was germinating. Even after all that God had done for me, I was doubting His existence and questioning if there was even a devil.

"The fool hath said in his heart, there is no God. They are corrupt, they have done abominable works, there is none that doeth good." (Psalms 14:1).

To anchor His attack, the devil sent another person to send me careening in the pit of doubt. This time, it was my cousin. He was purporting the validity of science and questioning the existence of God. I said to myself, this is the third time I've heard someone claiming that God does not exist. Could this be true? Entrapped in the enemy's snare, I got so depressed.

I wanted to believe in God, but I was questioning His existence.

One morning, as I was sleeping, an evil presence overcasted me, and all I could hear in my mind was, "There's no God." I tried to pray, but I could not. I fainted. All my strength was gone. I was burdened with a sense of significant loss. I got up, rushed to my grandmother, and called, "Grandma, Grandma!" But I was lost for words. I didn't know what to tell her. I got the feeling of grief and hopelessness that I felt when my father passed away. You could have touched me, and I would not feel it because I was numb.

My ministry in school began to sink. I was not as effective and excited about God as I was before. However, the Holy Spirit was on my case. Because of the experience I gained with God and the burning desire to save as many souls as possible, I was opened to His stirring, and thus, I pressed through the devil's snare and shared the Gospel with my fellow students. The hymn says, "From every stormy wind that blows, from every swelling tide of woes, there is a calm, a sure retreat: 'Tis found beneath the mercy seat." Furthermore, the word of God echoes, "And not only so, but we glory in tribulations also: knowing that tribulation worketh patience; And patience, experience; and experience, hope: And hope maketh not ashamed; because the love of God is shed abroad in our hearts by the Holy Ghost which is given unto us" (Romans 5:3-5).

I made it through Form 5 by the grace of God. For my graduation, I was awarded as the most disciplined student. I also received awards for perseverance, physical education, and sports. God had turned my life around. A student who was disrespectful to teachers and students became the most disciplined student; it had to be God. He pulled me from the pits of mocking, jeering, and being ill-mannered, rescuing me from the pits of doubt. Like Paul, He has called and chosen me to be His representative.

I believe God can do the same for you. By accepting Him into your life, He will transform you and make you a beacon of light to those who need Christ's transforming power. Moreover, He has a plan for your life. You may not see it now, but He has already mapped it out. Why not prove Him?

Meet Kimron Charles

Kimron is from the beautiful island of St. Vincent and the Grenadines, a country known for its many cultural attractions and unique black sand beaches.

He is a devoted Gospel worker who enjoys preaching, Bible study, and testimony. He delights in spreading the Gospel to as many people as possible. He serves at his local church as an elder, deacon, Sabbath school teacher, personal ministries secretary, publishing ministry coordinator, and interest coordinator.

His spiritual anchor is found in his favorite Bible Verse , Jude 1:24: "Now unto him that is able to keep you from falling, and to present you faultless before the presence of his glory with exceeding joy."

His mission is to see as many people saved in the Kingdom of God as possible.

CHAPTER 16

God Did not Forget Us

———— 66 ————

Can a woman forget her sucking child, that she should not have compassion on the son of her womb? yea, they may forget, yet will I not forget thee. Behold, I have graven thee upon the palms of my hands; thy walls are continually before me. Thy children shall make haste; thy destroyers and they that made thee waste shall go forth of thee. (Isaiah 49:15-17)

———— 99 ————

"What kind of a person brings children into a school library anyway? They are sleeping. A library isn't the place for that." Her words stung. I looked at her and then at my three little humans fast asleep on a chair in a corner of the school library. I fought back the tears. She would not have the privilege of seeing me cry. I would have told her where to go and how to get there on a typical day, but today was different. I could do nothing more than look at her. She then turned around, mumbling something to herself, and walked away. As I looked at these little humans, tears began to flow. I was a terrible mother, and I knew it. As my half-asleep, hungry babies and I made our way to the exit, I overheard the librarian saying to another staff, "She brought her siblings to the library, and they were over there sleeping." *I am their mother*, I thought, knowing had I said that it would be worse. I quickly ushered them out. *Is this ever going to get better?* I asked myself in anger. *Did she even know my situation? Would she even care?*

The rest of the evening was uneventful. We ate pasta for dinner, and the children's bedtime routine went seamlessly. Finally, I had some time for myself. I grabbed my pen and my book and began to write.

"Dear Jesus, what a day..."

I didn't have anyone to watch the children for me, and I was unwilling to leave them with anyone at the shelter, so I had to take them to school with me. I wished I could have called in, but I had an exam. I felt terrible waking them up at 4 am to catch the 5 am bus, especially since we only got to this shelter the night before and they didn't get much sleep. I was tired and watched them as they slept on the bus. My three little people. My Angel, my Rhain, and my Heaven. My eyes burned, and I couldn't focus enough to study on the bus for my exam. I looked out the window at the dark streets lit with streetlights and traffic signals. Two hours later, we arrived at the school.

They jumped off the bus, still half asleep and hungry. They ate at the cafeteria table, having some of the food I brought from the shelter. I watched them eat as they laughed, and we talked. I wished I was a better mother to them. They don't deserve this kind of life, running from shelter to shelter. This was our fifth shelter in the last two years.

It was almost time to get to my exam. I prepped them, as they would have to be in the library alone. "Don't yell or fight or go anywhere with anyone." They all agreed. "Mummy has to be in a different room, but I promise to come back and check on you." They were excited to be in college and couldn't wait to see what the library looked like. We entered what looked like a mansion of books to them. I allowed them to pick a quiet corner where they would not disturb the other students and stay out of view."

Angel was 9 years old at the time, Rhain 7, and Heaven 6. They were used to staying home alone, but this wasn't home. What if someone saw them and called the Children's Aid Society? We were just recovering from our last encounter with them, and the worker told me if he ever received another call, I would lose them for good this time.

I glanced at the wall clock; it was 5 minutes to exam time. I brushed off the thoughts and hugged my babies, reminding them to be good and sit nicely. They were obedient children, but they were still children. Heavy-heartedly, I went into the access center to do my exam. I've been struggling with test anxiety, major depression, and ADHD. These struggles awarded me accommodation to complete my exams in a separate room with extra time. As I sat anxiously waiting for my test paper, I prayed earnestly that they would be alright until I got back (as if getting back meant God no longer had to take care of them).

I was anxious that I couldn't focus on the questions asked. I just wanted to get back to my children. I don't know how or if I answered all the questions on the scantron, but I knew I was done in 15 minutes. I ran back to the library, and they were fast asleep, with books on their laps. I decided not to wake them but to quickly go to the washroom. On my way back, I saw the librarian standing close to them and looking around. I made it look like I was retrieving a book as I walked towards them. She then commented that children should not be in a school library, let alone sleeping in one. Did she have any idea what these children have been through? Has she the slightest clue that we were coming from a shelter and had been traveling since 5 am? Or that they were awake until 4 am the previous morning getting settled into their new "home?" Would she be more compassionate if she found out that I was a single mother trying to complete my diploma so that I could work and get them out of this situation? Did it even matter?

"I feel defeated, Lord." I was sexually molested by a female family friend, raped by another, and molested by another, all before the age of 9 years old. I've been on my own since I was 11 years old, sleeping in staircases, party rooms, homes of so-called friends, shelters, group homes, and foster care. I've been married and divorced. I'm currently married now, but that's not working out. I'm tired of dragging my children in and out of these shelters. They deserve better than this. The tears flowed as I looked at Angel and Rhain on their bunk bed. I then looked over at Heaven with a sad, heavy heart. I remembered Psalm 27:10 and decided that the best thing I could do for them was to give them up to foster care so they could have a home and some stability. God promised He would care for them if I left them. I wasn't leaving them. I had no job, no money, no car, no home. I wasn't a good mother, Lord, and I'm sorry.

I began to think about my childhood in Trinidad but could only remember bits and pieces. I remember living with my grandmother, aunt, and cousin, and my mother sent us barrels from Canada with the nicest clothes and shoes. I remember stealing money from my grandmother to impress the girls at school by buying them pizza in hopes they would like me and be my friend. I remember coming to Canada and how exciting it was to see snow. I remember being homeschooled for the first year because we didn't have proper documents to attend school. I remember having to leave the only home I knew in Canada. I remember staying with a "friend" and her family, only for her to destroy my clothes and shoes, drag my toothbrush across the carpet, and spread lies to our mutual friends about me.

I remember getting pregnant and wanting so much to have a baby but then losing it. I remember how dismissive and hurtful the father of my child was after I came home from the hospital. I remember feeling so alone during that miscarriage and having church people speak ill about me. I remember my ex-husband and father of my children putting his hands on me for the first time. I remember the first time he cheated on me. I remember being in the hospital alone after delivering our second and third child. I remember meeting my current husband and how the friend who encouraged me to date him was sleeping with my children's father and husband at the time. I remember my children's father leaving our daughter at daycare after being informed she was dangerously pyretic, only to go upstairs in the same building to visit that so-called friend of mine he was sleeping with. I remember having my children apprehended by Children's Aid and being gone for almost two years. I remember my current husband having 4 (to date) children outside of our relationship. I remember it all! But where were the good times?

I sat on the bed, feeling I wasn't worth much. I believed all of this happened to me because I did something wrong. I believed that by coming forward about the molestation, I had ruined my family, and God was repaying me for it. I began to lament all over again. I shouldn't have said anything; I mean, it wasn't that bad. It's not like it happened every night. Only sometimes, and I mean, wasn't it a good feeling? I was so depressed I didn't even realize the thoughts I permitted to enter and plant roots in my brain were poisoning my soul. Just then, the alarm went off. I was tired, but I hadn't even slept—time to get the little ones up and ready for the day.

The following days went by as a blur. I continued the mundane tasks of getting the children ready for the day and then for the night. While they were at school, I, too, was at school. We ate dinner and did our homework together at the shelter. I still held in the back of my mind that I should send them back to foster care, but I couldn't bring myself to make the call. I knew it would have been better for them, but selfishly, I couldn't let them go. They were all I had. Could anyone truly love them more than I could? Is the life I've exposed them to even love? I grappled with both.

I decided to leave the shelter and move back in with my husband. We lived in his bachelor apartment in a roach-infested building. At least the children would have a mother and father in the home, and we wouldn't be in a shelter. We didn't see eye to eye on most things. The main one was that he sold drugs out of the apartment. Every real gangster knows you don't work where you live and don't get high on your own supply. During an argument, he would remind me that I was living in his home. He was right. Prayerfully, my children and I hung on. I just needed to finish school and get a job in the nursing field.

One day, while grocery shopping, I received a phone call from a distant area code. When I answered, the lady on the other end, after confirming it was me, informed me that a 3-bedroom townhouse was available in a co-op complex. She informed me the unit was ready, and I could look at it to see if it was suitable for my children and me. She also said I could see it as soon as I was available. I couldn't believe my ears. I looked at the phone to make sure I wasn't hearing things.

"Hello, hello," I could hear her on the other end of the phone.

"Yes, I'm here," I responded. I was frozen. Was this really happening? I almost felt like it was some cruel joke.

"Jenna," I heard her say again.

"Yes, I'm so sorry," I responded.

"Who is this?"

She provided her name and the establishment from which she was calling. I accepted the offer to view the unit the following day.

My children and I were praying for certain things we desired in and around our home. God provided everything we asked Him for in this place. I was so excited to share with the children that we had our new place, but I decided to surprise them instead. I had a week to move all our items into the new home. That was more than enough time as we didn't have much. I asked my sister to keep them for the weekend, and I packed all their clothing and brought them into our new home. After praying and cleaning, I packed them all away.

I got them beds and mattresses that would be moved in before they were. The night we were to move in, there was an ice storm. I bundled my children up into my unsafe car and drove for 60 minutes to our new home. They kept asking, "Where are we going, Mommy?" But I would not tell them. I didn't have any pots yet, so we stopped and got some fast food. When we approached the complex, my daughter asked, "Who lives here, Mommy?" I told her someone she knew very well. Excitedly, they all leaped out of the car with their food in hand.

When we got to the door, I pretended I was ringing the doorbell while I unlocked it. I pushed the door open, and they walked in. They chorused, "Goodnight," but no one answered. They took their shoes off and waited for further instructions. I led them into the living room, which had no furniture.

My son said, "Mommy, I don't think anyone lives here."

I smiled at him and responded, "Of course, people live here."

He looked around at the space and asked, "Who?"

I smiled and responded with relief, "You do; we all do."

They stood silently for a few moments, looking at each other and then around, then yelled for joy. I didn't know the place or neighborhood, so I asked them to keep it down, or we may get kicked out. They asked if they could see upstairs. I reminded them this was their home, and they could go into any part they wanted. They checked out the rooms and were even more excited when they saw their beds and clothing in the rooms. We prayed and praised God that night.

I didn't have the best relationship with my father, but I now understand that he did his best with what he knew and had. I didn't see it that way back then. One day, he called me while I was at school and asked me to come see something he had just come across. I assumed it was some furniture as I had just moved, and being a contractor, he often got great items from his customers. I jotted down the address and headed there after my class. When I got there, it was a business place.

My father loves cars, and he always bought new ones every chance he got. I then realized it was a car dealership, and he found this beautiful black SUV he wanted to purchase. I looked at it, boy, was it ever fancy. It was the limited platinum edition of its class. In his excitement about the car, he began to share all the features of it with me. I caught on to his excitement. I had no idea, for the most part, what he was even talking about, but I was happy he asked my opinion and wanted to share this experience with me.

After confirming with me about 7 or 8 times If I genuinely approved of this new car purchase, he said, "Good, because it's for you." I didn't understand what he was saying. He had been telling me for years that he would buy me a car, and it never happened. Today was the day. The car I had was an old car, and the tires were bald. It had engine issues, and I would call him often to ask him how to mitigate one issue or another. He knew of the move and didn't find my car safe for traveling long distances with "his grandchildren." The following week, he showed up at our home with a complete living room set and some appliances. I couldn't believe it.

Five months later, I started my new job as a nurse in a hospital seven minutes away from my new home. My wait was long and painful. I can't tell how often I felt like giving up, but God's grace and mercy kept me. He did not forget me in my pit of desperation, desolation, and deprivation.

In my process of being mended by the Maker, like Leah, God did not forget me. Like Joseph, He uses people who caused us pain at times to help restore us. He hasn't forgotten you.

Meet Jenna Duncan

Jenna Duncan, a native of Trinidad and Tobago, is living proof that God uses what the enemy meant to harm for your good and His glory. God has blessed her in many ways with beauty throughout a life of what seemed like ashes. She is a mother of three, a life consultant, a speaker, and the founder of Mended by the Maker, a ministry that supports women of childhood sexual abuse. She has been gifted with a voice that she uses to minister in various churches in song. She is a writer of devotionals, which she shares on her website.

Jenna has been blessed with the unique gift to "heal the broken hearted," to "set at liberty those that are oppressed," and "recover of sight to the blind" (Luke 4:18). She is determined to live her life in a way to hear "Well done, thou good and faithful servant" (Matthew 25:21)

CHAPTER 17

Adherence to God's Instructions Brings Blessings

"

The Lord is my shepherd, I shall not want.
(Psalm 23:1)

"

For years, I struggled and fought desperately not to drown in my financial debts. I found myself in murky water, and like quicksand, I felt like all my efforts to escape proved futile. I slipped a little deeper with each attempt to get to the edge.

I learned that debt is one of the greatest antagonists to a Christian's progress. We live in an economic climate that requires monetary currency to survive. Everything we consume has a price tag, requiring frugality, self-regulation, and resourcefulness to thrive. Ecclesiastes 10:19 educates us that "Money answers all things." Therefore, unless we retreat into the wilderness to live a nomadic life, it is impossible to thrive in a developed society without access to some form of currency to trade for goods or services.

Many Christians delight in quoting 1 Timothy 6:10 as a warning against pursuing or desiring money, painting it as an evil device. Yet, even a church or a ministry needs money to be sustained. The key is having a healthy attitude towards it because, while God doesn't want us to make money an idol, He wishes us to live prosperous lives and have enough to care for ourselves, contribute to ministry, and bless others. Whether we care to acknowledge it, money is essential to a prosperous life, even to maintain good health.

God is the giver of wisdom, and like every area of life, He wants us to be good stewards of our resources. The failure to properly manage the resources God gave can thrust a well-intentioned Christian into a place of despondency and lack, leading them to live a substandard life, contrary to God's plan for us. As highlighted in the blessings listed in Deuteronomy 28, when God's children honor His commandments, He will make us the head and not the tail, lenders and not borrowers. It is not God's will for His children to be thrust into debt's depths. When we are financially distressed, it affects us emotionally, psychologically, and spiritually.

The Bible exhorts in Hebrews 13:5, "Keep your lives free from the love of money and be content with what you have, for God has said: Never will I leave you; never will I forsake you." This tells us that when we live within our means, steward our funds, and live a contented life, we need not struggle, clamor for loans, and put ourselves in financial crises.

After struggling to stay afloat in my pool of financial obligations and responsibilities for years, a time came when I thought that I would break free from debt. I was climbing the banks, holding onto the rails of stability, when I lost my footing and slipped back into its depths. My greatest fear was reaching retirement and still being saddled with debt. It seemed justifiable to keep borrowing when I needed raw cash to cover expenses or purchase something desperately needed—but the cycle was unending. It spiraled out of control, sending me into financial bankruptcy and embarrassment.

With minimal resources at my disposal and little support as a single mother, it was extremely difficult to balance my budget and stay financially buoyant. I worked a salary way below my expenses, and the bills and living incidentals kept mounting. When did it get to this? Where did I go wrong? How do I escape this murky trap?

Amid my financial predicament, I was attending university while my daughter was in high school, and both fees had to be paid along with other expenses, which included loans plus the usual upkeep. After wading tirelessly for years, I had finally maxed out, and my anxiety and worry peaked. I became numb and nonchalant and just moved around with the tide. My thoughts were, *let whatever happens happen*. I was acquainted with all the loan institutions; they knew me well. I would borrow from one loan agency to pay another, and the trend persisted. I was a chronic debtor, and my situation seemed hopeless.

To keep myself from going crazy, I kept occupied so I did not have to think about my dilemma. Sometimes, I was moving so fast that when the bills came, I felt as if I lingered a minute to think about them; I would go crazy, so I would enquire about all the loan places beforehand and secure a loan to take care of the impending expenditure and debts. My net salary had dwindled to almost zero, and I could not purchase the bare necessities.

When I had exhausted all the reputable loan facilities, I was drained of my physical and emotional energy and just floated in my pit, wondering what would become of me and my daughter. The withdrawals and deductions from my salary were so extreme I had nothing left for tithing. It plagued me that I had drifted so far that I felt not even God could help me. How could He, when I was robbing Him? This started to affect me emotionally, and I started having chronic headaches, especially during my pay period. Instead of relief, my income, or the lack of it thereof, brought depression. I had nothing to look forward to each month. I needed desperate intervention and transformation. I knew the blessings I should receive when I returned God's portion were in jeopardy. I felt guilty and worthless because I was not only failing myself and my daughter, but I was failing God.

Special occasions such as my daughter's birthday and mine left me feeling destitute and worthless. I could not treat or do anything special for her or myself. I deliberately pushed the thought of celebration from my mind. I would sit for hours thinking about ways I could get money to survive more comfortably, but my only recourse was through the aid of financial institutions. My pride would not allow me to seek the assistance of individuals like co-workers, church members, or family. I could not let anyone close to me know the extent of my crisis. I could not risk having anyone talking about me or looking down on me.

My daughter and I are very close, and even though I tried to shield and spare her the details of my predicament, she observed many things while growing up, and I thank God she has always been a thoughtful and contented child. I never felt pressured, even though I carried the guilt of not affording or providing the life she deserved. When she graduated high school, she sought a job to help me handle the household expenses. Although I desired more for her, she was adamant and decided not to matriculate to sixth form to do her CAPE subjects.

Even though I disagreed with her decision, I observed how sad she was when I mentioned borrowing money to further her studies, and it gave me pause. She persisted in her applications, eventually got a job at one of the most prominent institutions, worked there for a few years, and then applied to university. I acquired a one-time grant for her, which helped with part of her tuition fees. I was still studying part-time and had only a year left to my credit hours. Even though I felt like sacrificing my education to clear her path, I could not turn back; I needed to complete it to put me in a better position financially to acquire a job in my field. We pressed on, and within a year, I graduated and waited on God for a breakthrough in my career. It took three years before I got a solid job in my field of study, but it finally came.

After these three arduous years of waiting, wondering if I would make it out with my faculties intact, I transitioned into social work after graduating as a guidance counselor. I desired a positive and long-term change in my life that could lift me out of my financial instability, and God came through. I prayed day and night for His intervention, and despite my failures, He heard and delivered. I remember one night when my daughter was asleep. I cried to God as the tears flowed like a river. "God, you are my Shepherd, and you know my wants and, more so, my needs. Please help me from this foul position." I knew He heard my cry.

Even in the depths of my pit, I have always encouraged many individuals to cast all their cares on the Lord because He would sustain and never leave nor forsake them. I always wondered how I was able to be an encourager when I was drowning, and my circumstances seemed so hopeless. Was I being a hypocrite? Didn't these scriptural promises apply to me as well? I started questioning myself about my will to trust in God. Wasn't Micah 7:7 applicable to everyone? Shouldn't I be hopeful in the Lord and wait for Him? I was really in a bad state, and I needed urgent help. In addition to a lump sum of money to pay off my debt, I also needed a change of mindset and direction in handling my finances.

Shortly after being employed as a social worker, I got my appointment. My salary would be in a different category, and my gross would be more than what I was getting in my previous job. However, I had a mountain of debts looming over my head. It would take me some time, plus extreme discipline and consistency, to climb my way out of the murky waters, but things were looking up.

I had been robbing God of His portion for many years, and I was cognizant of the consequences. I repented and asked Him to give me a second chance. Despite the looming debts, I resolved to faithfully return God's portion each month, no matter how tight things got. It was challenging, but I needed a mustard seed to grow roots and take me out of my pit. Thus, I took out God's portion, and then I proceeded to pay the bills. Malachi 3:10 came as a warning and a blessing for me. God said I should bring all the tithes into his house and prove Him. He promised to open the windows of heaven and pour out a blessing. He declared there would not be enough room to receive this outpouring of blessing. I considered deeply the lesson it conveyed. I understood that blessings awaited me, and my barns would be filled when I acted in obedience. If I followed God's plan, I would never need to borrow or beg to survive, but I would have so much that I would not have room enough to receive it. The Lord spoke to me, and I was grateful.

The Holy Spirit spoke to me repeatedly in dreams, sermons, and conversations with individuals about tithes and offerings. This was a path towards reformation for me. I experienced a 180-degree shift in my life. Through discipline, dedication, and obedience, God delivered me from my financial woes and gave me a breakthrough.

I had cleared all my major debts and reached the point where I had a growing savings account. Things were looking up, but I was not fully clear of my challenges. After my financial reformation, I developed fibroids that caused me multiple health issues, which were unbearable after seeing numerous doctors and specialists who advised that I did a major surgery. Despite my pain and the inconvenience of purchasing medications and paying doctor bills, I was grateful that I was able to pay for my medications from savings accumulated after clearing most of my debts. Eventually, I had to come up with 1.5 million Jamaican dollars to do the major surgery and another 250,000 JMD for a minor surgery. The Lord extended His grace and mercy by allowing me to acquire a job that increased my income so I could take care of my living and medical expenses. Can you imagine if I had had these issues while I was drowning in debt? He cleared the way long before I got there.

He orchestrates and directs our paths when we obey His will. He is even a God of surprises, and He rewards diligence. For years, I was making overpayments to my mortgage and did not realize it. I believe God allowed this to happen so I could benefit in the long run. This facilitated a fast-forward payment on the plan so that I could complete payment years in advance and acquire my title before retirement. Additionally, I no longer have that deduction from my salary, which is a blessing.

While in my pit of financial crisis, God allowed me to take an introspective view and showed me how my poor financial habits had derailed my life. However, the greatest lesson I learned was the significance of faith and hope. These lessons were not forced upon me, but my experiences taught me how to submit to God's plan. They showed me the importance and the need to develop patience, and most importantly, they led me to a place of obedience and trust. God needed my full attention, and He showed me in a practical way how critical it is to be loyal and diligent in following His instructions.

I grew up in an environment where morning and evening worship were critical to life. During my economic troubles, I felt guilty about approaching God. I wasn't as diligent in my worship because I felt I had disappointed God. Without worship, I felt I was missing out on something essential. I was taught the principles of the Bible and knew that God is my Source. When we lose light of this, the enemy ensnares us and uses our challenges as a wedge between us and our God. But obedience is worship; when we do God's will, our blessing and prosperity are assured.

One of my favorite Scriptures is Psalm 23. It assures me that God is my Shepherd. Like a wandering sheep, I went grazing in treacherous fields, but God used His rod to correct me and His staff to pull me in and straighten my path gently. God never left my side even though I was committing a presumptuous sin. Philippians 1:6 assures that God will complete the good work He began in me on the day of Jesus Christ. I have learned invaluable lessons from my experiences, and I am a stronger Christian for it.

Developing stability in my finances was challenging, especially when the expenses were numerous, and my income was minimal. Since I have overcome this massive hurdle, I have learned that many others are encountering similar challenges. Despite our best intentions, because we are humans, our propensities lead us off course unless we are guided by the Holy Spirit and God's interventions. However, there is hope even in the most challenging times and circumstances. This hope is in Jesus, who will take over our finances and mindset and transform us to live according to His will for our lives.

He delivered me from the murky pit and can do the same for you.

Meet Evett James

Ms. Evett James's passion for counseling led her to pursue her Bachelor of Arts in Guidance and Counselling from the Jamaica Theological Seminary (JTS). She has also acquired certification in pre- and post-diagnostic counseling for HIV patients.

She is a medical social worker at the Bustamante Hospital for Children, where she works in the oncology unit, providing counseling support to cancer patients and their families. In addition to her fulfilling job, she also conducts weekly presentations on "Effective Parenting and Child Safety" at the outpatient department of Jamaica's only pediatric hospital.

Ms. James is the author of Encouragement—A Source of Strength for Life's Journey and Inspirational Healing—A Balm for Grieving Souls. *She is also co-author of* Waiting in the Pit Volume 2, *in which she chronicles her experiences with healing and forgiveness.*

She loves the arts and loves to sing, draw elements of nature, write poems, and write short plays. She is a storyteller and uses the previously mentioned media to empower others to uplift themselves.

CHAPTER 18

The Traumatized Man-Child

---------------- **"** ----------------

Search me, O God, and know my heart: Try me, and know my thoughts: And see if there be any wicked way in me, and lead me in the way everlasting (Psalm 139:23-24).

---------------- **"** ----------------

After watching a jaw-dropping presentation on narcism, my mind was left brimming with thoughts and questions I desired to expunge.

"What if I am a narcissist?"

"What if I am one and I am unaware?"

"What if I don't heal from it?"

Narcissism is currently a prevalent subject that has gained notoriety over the last few years. A lot has been discussed about it, yet not exhaustively.

Begun J (2023) defines narcism (NPD) as extreme self-involvement to the degree that it makes a person ignore the needs of those around them. He further states that while everyone may show occasional narcissistic behavior, true narcissists frequently disregard others or their feelings. They also do not understand the effect that their behavior has on other people.

Learning what this concept and its characteristics entail and experiencing it firsthand, I wished and prayed I was not plagued with this unfavorable affliction. Hence, I decided to take inventory of my life. I needed to understand my personality: thoughts, feelings, and behavior. Therefore, I resolved to be a student of my disposition. A difficult childhood and youth had left me emotionally scarred, and I was concerned that the after-effects may have left scar tissues that could affect how I treated and related to people.

I grew up in a luxurious household (by my cultural standards), but sadly, I often found myself a silent observer, navigating the complexities of my parents' busy double-income marriage. My father typified the hardworking provider and dedicated his days to pursuing financial stability. However, despite his physical presence, his emotional availability was limited, as his attention was divided between work and family dynamics.

In stark contrast, my mother wielded her influence with an iron fist, typified by what psychologists term "narcissistic tendencies." While she projected an image of warmth and resilience to the outside world, her actions at home revealed a different persona. Her insatiable need for validation led to emotional neglect, leaving me feeling like a mere spectator in my own life.

While growing up, I yearned for connection and affection, but my attempts to connect with my mother were met with cold indifference. Her attention was often consumed by her desires and insecurities, leaving me feeling alienated and unimportant.

The impact of my mother's self-absorption affected my formative years, leaving an indelible mark on my psyche. Her egotism and emotional detachment created a toxic environment within our household, characterized by a conspicuous absence of the nurturing warmth critical for healthy child-rearing.

As the middle child, I found myself particularly vulnerable to the effects of my mother's neglect, often bearing the brunt of her indifference and self-centeredness. While my siblings each coped in their distinct ways, I struggled to find solace or validation within the emotional void created by her self-absorbed tendencies. This sense of emotional isolation and neglect deeply impacted my sense of self-worth and belonging, shaping my understanding of love, empathy, and resilience in several ways. The familial dynamics shaped by my mother's propensities laid the groundwork for a chaotic road to self-discovery and my healing, one fraught with a relentless quest for connection and emotional fulfillment.

Dr. Jordan Peterson, a distinguished psychologist, provides valuable insights into the intricate dynamics of child psychology, shedding light on the profound impact of emotional neglect on individuals like me. He greatly emphasizes the significant role of a nurturing parent-child bond in fostering healthy emotional growth during childhood. The absence of such nurturing led to substantial challenges in forming secure attachments and managing interpersonal relationships. Without the emotional support and guidance needed to develop a strong sense of self-worth and belonging, I grappled with feelings of isolation and inadequacy. Dr. Peterson's insights underscore the long-lasting effects of emotional neglect, highlighting the importance of early intervention and supportive environments in promoting positive emotional development.

Over time, I developed a distorted perception of self, hampering my ability to form meaningful connections. Navigating my mother's indifference became a significant challenge, shaping my understanding of love, empathy, and resilience for years.

Besides these emotional and psychological challenges, I also had physical health challenges during my childhood. My early life was overshadowed by frequent visits to hospitals, where sickness became a constant unwelcome friend from the moment I was born. From birth, I was vulnerable and frail and was accustomed to the sterile confines of hospital wards at infancy while my age mates reveled in the joys of preschool and nursery school. I had anemia and asthma, and these ailments never ceased to remind my parents of my fragile state. Yet, it was the obstinate wounds and sores covering my legs that posed the greatest threat to my well-being. Despite numerous treatment attempts, they resisted healing. My father, driven by a parent's relentless love, spared no effort in seeking treatment for these stubborn sores, yet despair lingered as the specter of amputation loomed.

In the face of conflicting emotions, my parents were thrust into a distressing decision-making process characterized by uncertainty and fear. Their brittle hope clung desperately to prayers for a miracle that could spare their son from a life of potential permanent disability and hardship. Against all odds, their prayers were answered with an incredible finding of a new medication, which became a catalyst for a significant turning point in my leg wounds and sores. With the administration of this groundbreaking treatment, a ray of hope pierced through the darkness of despair that had wrapped my family. My legs, once on the precipice of irreversible loss, began to respond positively to the medication's effects, signaling a notable shift in my health trajectory. As the threat of amputation slowly dissipated, replaced by gradual healing and restoration, I was now filled with a newfound sense of optimism and relatively good health.

When I transitioned into primary school, I faced fresh challenges from my unconventional upbringing. Skipping the typical preschool or nursery experience, I carried the weight of past struggles with me as I ventured into this new chapter of my life. Given my delicate health, battling anemia and asthma, doctors had given me stringent precautions against physical exertion. These precautions greatly robbed me of the quintessential childhood activities that fostered interpersonal skills and friendships among my peers. Deprived of the joys of sports, picnics, and school trips, I explored the terrain of primary school with an acute sense of caution and care, always mindful of my limitations and vulnerabilities.

For the most part, the absence of typical childhood experiences not only isolated me from my peers but also worsened my sense of difference and alienation. This further complicated my emotions and distorted my fragile sense of self-worth. In the absence of these formative experiences, I found myself wrestling with a great sense of inadequacy and detachment, setting the stage for a challenging road to self-discovery amidst the confines of an unforgiving environment.

Psychologists underscore the negative repercussions of social exclusion during childhood, something I experienced firsthand. Exclusion from typical childhood activities such as playing with peers, taking part in school trips, and engaging in sports can have enduring emotional and psychological effects. According to prominent psychologist Jean Piaget, "Play is the work of childhood," underlining the significant role of play in a child's development. Because I was deprived of these opportunities, I missed out on indispensable experiences for building social skills and forming meaningful bonds. Also, social exclusion is associated with increased feelings of loneliness, depression, and anxiety, as observed by psychiatrist Viktor Frankl, who stated, "An abnormal reaction to an abnormal situation is normal behavior." This means emotional distress experienced by socially excluded children is a natural response to their circumstances.

Studies also suggest that children who endure social exclusion often struggle with low self-esteem and forming meaningful relationships later in life. Developmental psychologist Erik Erikson states, "Children love and want to be loved, and they prefer the joy of accomplishment to the triumph of hateful failure." Not having social interaction also obstructs the development of vital social skills like empathy and communication, as noted by psychologist Daniel Goleman, who said, "Empathy begins with understanding life from another person's perspective. Nobody has an objective experience of reality." Children may struggle to understand others' perspectives and communicate effectively without opportunities to interact fully with peers. This impedes their ability to form healthy relationships in adulthood.

My ordeal was saturated with the lack of emotional support both at home and in my social environment, which escalated my emotional struggles. Notably, the lack of nurturing care from my mother and my exclusion from typical childhood experiences deepened my sense of isolation and alienation. I was deprived of the considerate care that is essential for a child's emotional development. My extreme bashfulness and shyness made it even more challenging for me to seek solace or support from others. My isolation was not by choice but a consequence of my circumstances, leaving me longing for connection and understanding.

With a limited supportive family environment and adequate emotional care, I faced an uphill battle in dealing with emotions and forming secure attachments. Maya Angelou once remarked, "I sustain myself with the love of family." Regrettably, the love and support that should have sustained me were conspicuously absent, leaving a void that echoed in my childhood.

While my father tried to remain steadfast in his support, embodying the compassion and grace that reflect the divine love taught in the Christian faith, it was not sufficient to fill the void left by my mother's emotional neglect. As Mother Teresa once said, "I have found the paradox that if you love until it hurts, there can be no more hurt, only more love." My father demonstrated selfless love, but the emotional nurturing traditionally associated with maternal care was absent. This echoes the sentiment expressed by Saint Teresa of Calcutta, who accentuated the importance of maternal love in nurturing children and shaping their emotional well-being. Yes, men are capable of providing emotional warmth and care, but their approach to parenting often differs from that of women due to societal expectations and gender norms.

My early lived experiences and emotional neglect resulted in cognitive dissonance, a psychological phenomenon where contradictory thoughts or beliefs coexist, leading to confusion and a desire to resolve the inconsistency. Growing up in an environment where my mother's emotional unavailability clashed with my father's love and support, I grappled with conflicting emotions and beliefs. This internal conflict often left me paralyzed by self-doubt and second-guessing my decisions as I struggled to reconcile the contrasting dynamics within my family. Cognitive psychologist Leon Festinger noted, "People strive for internal consistency to reduce cognitive dissonance, which causes mental discomfort." For me, this meant struggling with a constant battle between longing for my mother's affection and the reality of her emotional neglect, compounded by her overt favoritism towards my siblings.

The favoritism I experienced at home further worsened my emotional struggles and challenged my sense of self-worth. My mother's blatant preference for my elder brother and younger sister left me feeling overlooked and undervalued, overshadowing my achievements and contributions within the family. My mother's favoritism not only strained my relationship with her but also affected my education and overall well-being. Despite these challenges, I found solace and stability in my relationship with my father.

During the transitional period when my father retired from employment so that he could focus on farming, I experienced a whirlwind of changes that significantly impacted my mental, emotional, and educational well-being. With my father's diminished presence in the family structure and my mother assuming the role of the sole breadwinner, a power shift occurred within the household dynamics. While my mother wielded financial control, I found solace and acceptance in my father's nurturing presence, feeling truly seen and heard in his company. This forced me to relocate to live with my father at the farm.

Despite the challenges of cycling 50 kilometers to school each day, I found resilience in the love and support I experienced within the nurturing environment of the farm. Even with a history of having asthma, I found myself participating in physical activities, including cycling and even soccer, defying the constraints of my health conditions and self-disbelief.

Amidst my struggles, I encountered a transformative experience when I was introduced to the book "Ministry of Healing" by Ellen G. White. This encounter sparked further cognitive dissonance within me as I grappled with the teachings promoting a vegetarian diet. Despite initial skepticism and my mother's disbelief, I resolved to take on vegetarianism, guided by my newfound understanding of health and spirituality. The decision to adopt a vegetarian diet brought about a revolution in my health and well-being. Freed from the constraints of physical health challenges, I fully participated in sports and school activities, experiencing newfound confidence and self-esteem. My journey from cognitive dissonance to embracing a vegetarian lifestyle not only transformed my physical health but also deepened my spiritual connection, paving the way for a brighter future despite my challenging upbringing.

Despite my academic prowess, I faced significant barriers to accessing higher education due to financial constraints and my mother's favoritism towards my siblings. The death of my father further aggravated my emotional turmoil, stripping away my primary source of support and leaving me feeling isolated and alone in the world.

Due to my strained relationship with my mother, my academic pursuits were hindered by financial instability. I then found solace and strength in my faith. Turning to God for guidance and support, I immersed myself in church activities, seeking refuge in prayer and spiritual connection. However, my dreams of ministering and serving others seemed like distant aspirations for a shy and persecuted young man grappling with trauma and depression.

Then, amidst the darkness, a glimmer of hope emerged as I found a sense of purpose and belonging in literature evangelism. Encouraged by a prominent church leader, I took a leap of faith and enrolled at Rusangu University to study theology. This pivotal moment marked a turning point in my life, offering me a path toward healing and self-discovery as I embraced my calling and found the strength to overcome my emotional and mental struggles. Through perseverance and faith, I transformed my challenges into opportunities for growth and redemption, ultimately finding fulfillment in my journey toward becoming a preacher and serving others through his ministry.

"I PRESS ON" (Philippians 3:13,14)

Paul knew it was impossible to produce different results while being the same person. The only way this process of metamorphosis could happen was when "the locus of control" was internal and not external. The mind had to be disciplined and trained to focus on the desired goal. He uses the word "forgetting" to signify a process of repression and mindfulness—deliberately resisting negative emotions and thoughts and focusing on the positive by the grace of God. He uses the word "press" to indicate that it's impossible to casually move into the future.

Neuroscientists claim that the subconscious mind controls 95 % of a person's behavior and 5% of the conscious mind. Much of what we see people do is done on autopilot (subconsciously). In other words, the brain is a memory of the past, and what is often exhibited daily is the "program" of the subconscious mind. The beauty is the subconscious cannot tell between the real and the unreal. This means that we can set goals deliberately daily to rewire the subconscious. Daily affirmations, journaling, prayer, study, and meditation on God's word mindfulness will ensure that the set of our mind is altered.

Therefore, it will require us to treat each day as a new one, never relying on past experience, glory, or victory.

The songwriter could only say:

"Or if, on joyful wing cleaving the sky

Sun, moon, and stars forgot, upward I fly

Still, all my songs shall be

Nearer, my God, to thee

Nearer, my God, to thee, nearer to thee!"

Today, I stand as a living testament to the miraculous power of God's love and redemption. Through the valleys and pits of despair and the shadows of brokenness, I have walked, guided by the hand of the Almighty, to emerge on the other side as a preacher of righteousness and truth. In my life, I have experienced the transformative grace of Jesus Christ firsthand. As it says in 2 Corinthians 5:17, "Therefore, if anyone is in Christ, he is a new creation. The old has passed away; behold, the new has come." Indeed, I stand before you as a new creation, healed and washed clean by the blood of the Lamb and filled with the light of His love.

In the quiet moments of prayer, I am reminded of the words of Jeremiah 29:11, "For I know the plans I have for you, declares the Lord, plans for welfare and not for evil, to give you a future and a hope." With this promise etched in my heart, I continue to minister to those in need, offering hope and restoration through the power of God's love. It was the power of love that helped me release resentment for my mother.

For years, I couldn't understand why my mother treated me the way she did. It was not until after I learned about her story and connected it to my adversity that I understood that her behavior was that of a suffering person. She was severely tortured mentally by a dad who did not accept her as a female.

I discovered that Mom's dad desired a male child for his firstborn. Unfortunately, he got a little girl instead. To make matters worse, he verbalized his preference and subsequent disappointment, and she learned about it. This could have caused her to feel rejected and assume a masculine role to win his approval.

In many African cultures, the firstborn child symbolizes legacy, leadership, responsibility, cultural preservation, and family pride. The firstborn is often a source of pride for the family, symbolizing their strength and continuity. Please note that these symbolisms vary across different African cultures. Gender roles and expectations are now evolving, and not all cultures emphasize the concept of a male firstborn child.

However, this was my mother's reality, and she was trying very hard to be the male child dad did not have without realizing how it affected her personality and relations with others, especially her children. I have now learned to put everything in context and decided to forgive her and accept her as a person who also needs to heal from her childhood trauma. I no longer hold any anger or grudges against her.

As a district pastor, I use my experience and upbringing as a catalyst to help children and young people who may be enduring childhood trauma and parental neglect. I use my ministry to ensure that the children's ministry departments have the resources and attention that could help equip the children for their growth process. I make time to speak to them by guiding and encouraging them to be self-reliant and develop problem-solving skills. Empathy and active listening are vital to building connections with children; it gives them an opportunity to communicate their challenges. I also deliberately engage in playful activities fostering joy, creativity, and connection.

As a father, I pay special attention to my children's needs and spend time learning, unlearning, and relearning as I navigate the terrains of parenthood and family dynamics. One critical thing I have learned is to treat other people's kids as my own, as I am ever aware of how an adult's actions and inactions can affect a child's psyche.

From my pit, I have learned resilience, empathy, and compassion. By the grace of God and the working of the Holy Spirit, I emerged better, not bitter. I am determined to use my experience as a steppingstone to bring awareness and help both parents and children emerge from the pits of narcissistic tendencies, parental neglect, and childhood trauma.

As we journey together, may we find solace in the comforting embrace of our Heavenly Father, knowing that He is with us always, guiding us toward a future filled with hope and abundant blessings. Through prayer, counseling, and a steadfast commitment to a positive mindset rooted in the promises of God's Word, we continue to witness the incredible power of healing and restoration in the lives of countless souls. As I extend my hand to you today, I invite you to join me on this journey of faith, to experience the overwhelming grace and mercy of our Savior, Jesus Christ. Let us walk together in the light of His love by faith and not emotions, "for in him we live and move and have our being" (Acts 17:28 NIV).

Meet G.C

The author, a mental health advocate, missionary, and pastor from the beautiful continent of Africa, would like to remain anonymous to protect his and his family's identity. He desires that his story will raise awareness and bring hope to someone who may have or is going through the challenges he endured as a child.

CHAPTER 19

Saved From the Pit of Homelessness

―――――――― **"** ――――――――

*But my God shall supply all your need, according to His riches in glory, by Christ Jesus (**Philippians 4:19**).*

―――――――― **"** ――――――――

It is every couple's dream to own a home. If they did not accomplish this feat while they were single, it would be one of their foremost and significant goals to achieve as a unit.

After getting married at the age of twenty-six, I also had a dream of acquiring a home with my husband. However, we encountered many challenges after moving from the country to the city. Only a few months after our nuptials, my husband lost his job, and we had to give up the home we had planned on renting. Soon, we were living with my dad, who was pleading for months for me to return to live with him. We decided that irrespective of the challenges, we would press on, trust God, and continue seeking employment. Giving up was never an option for us.

"Have I not commanded you? Be strong and courageous. Do not be afraid; do not be discouraged, for the Lord your God will be with you wherever you go" (Joshua 1:9).

Just as God promised, we both successfully acquired jobs not long after. We decided that we would save as best as possible and apply for a loan to purchase our first home. However, various applications to the National Housing Trust for home acquisition within their housing schemes proved futile. From the large pool of applicants, they preferred granting more mature applicants who had further mileage in the labor field. We did not have enough hair under our working chins.

The years went by, and things became more and more challenging as we had previously expanded our family through procreation. Our children grew, and space became increasingly limited at my father's home. We never intended to venture into a rented home after leaving there. The plan was to move into our newly purchased home. However, family issues arose, and urgent decisions had to be made. The idea of moving straight into our house began to look improbable each day as our continuous attempts with the Housing Trust failed. As things escalated, we had little option but to move into a rented space. We were also hoping that wherever we rented, we had the prospect of purchase. However, the landlord informed us that her brother partly owned it and wasn't desirous of selling it. Still, the Lord in His Word reminded us: "But they that wait upon the Lord shall renew their strength; they shall mount up with wings as eagles..." (Isaiah 40:31). At this point, the wait was inevitable.

As a young couple with an average income, managing the bills was never easy, but the Lord would always make a way. My husband exhibited the characteristics of a diligent provider and shouldered most of the responsibilities in many areas. At the same time, I worked and studied concurrently, took care of my dad's financial expenses, and assisted some of my siblings and other relatives. Sometimes, the responsibilities and expenditures became overwhelming, but God kept us going. He is never slack concerning His promises, and thus He proved His words in Psalm 34:10: "The lions may grow weak and hungry, but those who seek the Lord lack no good thing."

One day, the landlord visited the house to inform me that her brother was coming from the U.S. and needed the use of the house, so we had to leave promptly. She said that they were trying to make other arrangements for us, but it did not work out. As she spoke, the Holy Spirit prompted me to pray. Without hesitation, I went into my bedroom, covered my head, knelt at the foot of my bed where I would often pray, and talked to my heavenly Father. My husband had gone on a vacation. Before I called him, a sudden, inexplicable peace came over my soul. Immediately, I trusted God would make a way, even though I didn't know what He had in store.

"I will even make a way in the wilderness and rivers in the desert. The beast of the field shall honor me, the dragons and the owls: because I give waters in the wilderness and rivers in the desert, to give drink to my people, my chosen" (Isaiah 43:19-21).

After getting off my knees, I called my husband and told him what had transpired. He told me to check the classified ads for any house available for rent. I was also led to call one of my church elders and mentor, along with two of my best friends from work, Rose and Carmalita. Rose told me she would take the Sunday Gleaner to work the following day so I could also look through it.

Monday morning, while on a break at work, I scanned through the pages of the classified ads and made calls. I discovered that all the houses listed for rental in and around the area had already been taken. After making the last call, my eyes caught something inexplicable; right there on the page before me, a bright light shone and encircled an entry.

It was a three-bedroom house with two bathrooms, a kitchen, dining room, living room, and washroom. What was most noticeable at the time was that this house wasn't for rent; it was for sale. I was captivated and awed by the bright light around this ad, and I started envisioning what it looked like based on its description. I was then roused by the realization that we had no money to buy a home. I had just completed my university studies, for which I had depleted all our savings, and my salary had not yet been increased to reflect my higher level of accreditation. Just then, a still, small voice penetrated all the thoughts floating around my head, "Call the number." I hesitated. *Call the number.* How am I going to call to purchase a home, especially one of that size, without money? Still, the small, gentle voice repeated, "Call the number."

Instead of calling the number, I went downstairs to Carmallita's classroom, showed her the entry in the Gleaner, and told her about the bright light that shone around it. She was excited as she uttered, "Steph, this looks really nice; call the number."

"But how can I when I don't know where the money will come from?" I responded.

"Steph, call the number!" she insisted.

"Now faith is the substance of things hoped for, the evidence of things not seen" (Hebrews 11:1).

As I went back up the stairs and thought about what was happening, I felt like I was in a daze. I knew I had to call, and I did. The pleasantness of the voice on the receiving end of the phone was like music to the ear. Mrs. Mann warmly introduced herself and asked if I would like to view the home that afternoon. She told me she was unable to meet me there that afternoon, but I could go and view the exterior, and if I liked it, she would meet me there and have me view the interior the following morning before work. I agreed instantly.

That evening, I went on a mission to locate the house. I walked around the entire community, back and forth, unable to find the house. I later discovered that I had passed it several times without realizing it. This was another test of my faith. Even though I did not get to view the exterior, I called Mrs. Mann and told her I would like to view the inside the following day. As I set out early the next morning, I realized the house was closer than I had thought. As I stepped into the yard, something beckoned me to go straight to the back. I immediately found solace beneath a big mango and some ackee trees towering over me. As I sat waiting for Mrs. Mann, I heard the same still, calm, gentle, reassuring voice whisper, "This home belongs to you." I started to soak in the blessed assurance with greater belief than before.

Mrs. Mann soon came and opened the house for me to inspect. The inside was even more beautiful than the outside, with closets, ceiling fans, and stunning fixtures. It also had a water tank and was only going for seven million Jamaican dollars, less than USD 40,000.00. As she sat on the stairs leading from the dining room going up into the kitchen (which became one of my favorite parts of the house), Mrs. Mann looked at me with a warm smile and said, "I have three other potential buyers who are willing to buy cash, but there is just something about you." I smiled back hesitantly, as I knew I had no money at all. She said, "Do you have money, Stephanie?" I replied, "No..." in a reluctant, soft tone, "but the Lord *will* make a way."

I told her I would be applying for a loan at the National Housing Trust. This idea came to my mind right there on the spot. Unexpectedly, Mrs. Mann looked at me reassuringly and replied, "I will wait for you." I fought hard to hold back the shock that crept up my cheeks. How could you turn down three cash buyers to wait on someone to get a loan, which would take time and more? The Lord was indeed working on my behalf.

"At the right time, I, the Lord, will make it happen" (Isaiah 60:22).

As I proceeded with audacious faith to acquire this seemingly impossible dream, I found that there were necessary legal documents that needed to be taken care of when purchasing a home. There were documents such as a surveyor's ID and an evaluation report, in addition to getting a lawyer to handle all the legalities and so on. Being a well-experienced real estate agent for years, Mrs. Mann assisted me in accomplishing these at far less than the average market prices. Whenever a transaction needed my attention, she would pick me up (as I had no personal ride then) to take care of them and drop me off for work on time. She also negotiated the best deals on our behalf.

Mrs. Mann wasn't the only good Samaritan God sent our way. We needed aid to ascertain the loan for a down payment on the property in terms of collateral. My friends from church, Mr. and Mrs. Brown, tendered their titles so that we could get the down payment and other finances for the paperwork and legalities to take to the National Housing Trust (NHT). They had never done anything like this before or even considered it, but they said, "Stephy, you have always been helping us, so it's nothing for us to help you."

"Give, and it shall be given unto you; good measure, pressed down, shaken together, and running over, shall men give into your bosom. For with the same measure that ye mete withal it shall be measured to you again" (Luke 6:38).

In no time, all the prerequisites were taken care of, and glory to God, the loan was granted. When he returned, my husband only needed to sign off on the agreement to share in the mortgage. As I recall, this wasn't the only miracle that the Lord blessed us with. While waiting to process the loan at the NHT, in January of 2013, Mrs. Mann called me while

I was at work one day and said, "Stephanie, tell me something; where you are living now, are you still paying rent?" I responded, "Yes, Mrs. Mann."

All the processing would be completed by July of that year, and the NHT would then pay her the purchasing cost of the house. My landlady and her brother were waiting impatiently to occupy their home and kept asking when we would move out. Mrs. Mann said, "I'm coming to your workplace to give you something." When she got there, she handed me the keys and said, "Here are the keys to your home. You do not need to pay rent anymore." I was in total awe. "How God?" This was one of the best, most rewarding, and accomplished feelings I had ever experienced.

We moved into our home before paying a dime one day before our twelfth wedding anniversary. We saved six months of rental payments. The Lord inspired Mrs. Mann to bestow upon us this uncommon favor! "For the Lord God is a sun and shield; The Lord bestows favor and honor; no good thing does He withhold from those whose walk is blameless" (Psalm 84:11). I was far from blameless, and still am, yet the Lord chose to lavish us with His beautiful blessings in miraculous ways.

I said to Him, "This home will be a ministry for you." It has been eleven years since God has blessed me with this home. Countless students and other children and relatives have been blessed by it. It has been a house of hospitality, worship, and prayer. Many have found shelter, a place of refuge, comfort, and safety within its walls. Many miracles and testimonies were birthed within its humble perimeters, and I give God all honor and glory. Even though I have experienced many challenges of ill-health and marital attacks, as I outlined in *Waiting in the Pit 2*, I have so much to rejoice for because of the miracles God has wrought in my life. Chief among my blessings is this miraculous acquisition when God saved me from homelessness.

My friend, God is faithful and worth serving. Be assured that whatever pit you have found yourself immersed in, "At the right time, I, the Lord, will make it happen" (Isaiah 60:22). He did it for me and can do it for you, too.

Meet Stephanie Minto-Hinds

Stephanie Minto-Hinds has been a devoted Christian for almost her entire life. She has experienced mighty miracles at the hand of God after going through extenuating circumstances, challenges, and experiences.

Stephanie has been a teacher for over twenty years and holds a Diploma in Teacher Education, a Bachelor of Arts Degree in Education and Literacy (honors), and a tentative master's degree in Curriculum Development.

As an experienced teacher, Stephanie is blessed with the grand opportunity to share the love and marvelous works of the Lord with students, parents, and other stakeholders alike. She desires to keep letting others taste and see God's goodness and that nothing is impossible with and through Him.

Stephanie has been married for over twenty years. She has proven that with God, unconditional love, and forgiveness, you can navigate any tests that can potentially attack and destroy your marriage or any aspect of your life, as she would have shared via co-authoring in Waiting in the Pit 2.

She is the proud mother of two adult children, a lawyer, and an aspiring cardiothoracic surgeon.

CHAPTER 20

Rest Assured in God's Love

"

There is no fear in love; perfect love drives out all fear. So then, love has not been made perfect in anyone who is afraid, because fear has to do with punishment. **(1 John 4:18)**

"

As I converse with friends and people I meet, a common view shared is that life seems to rush us by. The 24-hour day, 7-day week, and the 12 months of the year have not changed. However, our lives are becoming busier, and the days seem shorter. During the weekdays, as soon as I wake up in the early hours of the morning, I hear in my mind,

Ready, steady, go go go! My usual routine includes preparing my children and then traveling to and from school, work, food shopping, and completing home duties. Thus, often, you would find me running for the buses to make it from point A to B, then C and D. There are days when I feel like I am running a marathon, and therefore, I long for an opportunity to rest. Over time, I have learned to seek more of God's help to complete my responsibilities, and I am thankful that "my help comes from the Lord, the Maker of heaven and earth" (Psalm 121:2).

From an early age, I have always deeply loved children. My love and joy for children multiplied in September 2015 when I held my first-born son, David. It was the most beautiful moment ever in my life. His radiant beauty instantly sparked an unexpected explosion of love within me, unlike anything I had known before. My excitement and joy were once again renewed in December 2017 when God gifted me my second-born son, Josiah. As I held him in my arms, I fell deeply in love with him. He was beautiful in every way, and I praised God for His protection over our lives. In November 2020, I received another miracle gift when my third-born son, Solomon, was born. As I held my beloved son in my arms, I gazed upon his beauty, and my heart overflowed with love. I was in awe of God's favor upon our lives.

God chose my sons' names; I call them my young kings. My sons are my most precious blessings and miracles; they represent the miraculous beauty that God can extract from the most unseemly, unsightly, and unfavorable circumstances. They are my lilies that emerged from murky waters, my diamonds from the dark depths, and my silk from worm cocoons. Their presence in my life is a tangible manifestation and assurance of God's love, mercy, and grace. They are a constant reminder that God's love for me is infinite and that He does not hold my past sins and indiscretions against me.

Having grown up in a Christian home, I embraced biblical values and principles, including the value of marriage and family life. From childhood, I understood that God ordained marriage. I have always been amazed and inspired by how God had orchestrated the most beautiful love story since the creation of Adam and Eve (Genesis 22:21-23). I have also admired and appreciated my parents' marriage; they have been married for 33 years. One of my favorite memories is a beautiful picture of Dad teaching Mum how to ride a bike while they laughed and spent quality time together. Another favorite memory they shared with us was when they planted flowers and vegetable gardens together in their first home. My parents' positive example influenced me to pray and seek God's help as I waited for a husband.

Before becoming a mother, I had a draft plan for my life.

Step 1: Complete my college A-level studies and then enroll in university, with an ambition to graduate at twenty-three.

Step 2: Search for graduate jobs and transition into employment for about two years.

Step 3: Start a family before the age of thirty.

It was my prayer to find the love of my life between the ages of 23 to 25. We would spend time to get to know each other before marriage, then spend what I call an "extended honeymoon period" before the blessing of children. I envisioned a beautiful life ahead. I believe that God would have answered my prayers, but sometimes, our plans do not always go the way we desire, even with the best of intentions. As we travel on life's highway, we sometimes come across speed bumps and even road spikes, puncturing our dreams and derailing our plans, sending us careening into pits and ditches.

As I contemplate, I am drawn back to a memorable experience in 2023 when I watched the Christian movie "Overcomer" on Netflix. The movie left an indelible impression on me, and it caused me to reflect deeply on my life experiences and my journey of motherhood thus far. In particular, the following conversation was very significant and an inspiration for my story:

Tomas: John, if I ask you, "Who are you?" What's the first thing that comes to mind?

John: I am a basketball coach.

Tomas: And what if that is stripped away?

John: I am also a history teacher.

Tomas: If we take that away, who are you?

John: Well, I'm a husband. I'm a father.

Tomas: And God forbid that should ever change. Who are you?

John: I don't understand this game.

Tomas: It is not a game, man. Who are you?

John: I'm… I'm a white American male.

Tomas: Yeah, that's for sure? Is there anything else?

John: Well, I'm a Christian.

As the conversation continued, Tomas said something to John which caught my attention; *"Your identity will be tied to whatever you give your heart to."* This profound statement touched my heart and troubled my soul to such a degree that rivulets of tears began to stream down my cheeks.

As I watched the movie, I answered the questions silently. Like John, my identity was intertwined with my most important role as a mother and other responsibilities. However, I continued pondering the questions and wanted to know who I truly was. Many thoughts flooded my mind. I became overwhelmed with emotions because I slowly realized that I was no longer sure of who I was. My search for answers reminded me of some difficult experiences I had endured and gone through in the past years of motherhood. My heart was broken, and my spirit grieved the deep pain of being a victim of emotional, financial, sexual, and spiritual abuse. I constantly questioned myself: what had I done to deserve such treatment? I often blamed myself in my state of hopelessness, and sometimes, the enemy convinced me that I deserved the ill treatment.

Where did it all start?

One warm summer evening, as I was traveling by bus to an African food store, where I usually shop for food items not commonly sold in my hometown, my olfactory senses picked up a whiff akin to barbequed chicken. It was as if the aroma was beckoning to me. I was puzzled because this was a bustling shopping street. When the bus stopped at the traffic lights, I noticed a man turning chicken on a big barbequing drum just outside a Jamaican takeout restaurant. I had never seen a Jamaican restaurant in the area before, so after I had finished my food shopping, I decided to go back and discover what I might have been missing.

Upon entering the establishment, I was greeted with a friendly attitude and a strong accent as the shopkeeper asked what I would like to order. I explained that I was there for the first time and asked a few questions about the menu and the food on display. For my story, I will call the shopkeeper,

Leonard. Leonard tried to explain the different dishes, but because I was not accustomed to Jamaican cuisine or culture, I decided to try something simple and ordered two dumplings. As I waited, I enjoyed the lively music even though I couldn't understand everything being said. After a few minutes, I received my order, but Leonard also kindly added a portion of rice and peas with chicken so I could sample something more filling. I thanked him for his kindness. As I was about to leave, I impulsively asked whether a part-time job was available. He took my contact details and explained that he was both the chef and the operations manager, so he would contact me as soon as there was a vacancy.

About a week later, I received a call and was offered a part-time job. Within a month, I had become familiar with the restaurant's operations and the food. Leonard and I maintained a good working relationship. I started enjoying some of the spicy foods on the menu, including jerked chicken, ackee, and saltfish, but dumplings remained among my favorites.

After working together for about two months, Leonard and I started to spend time together after work and slowly built a much closer bond. Leonard began to express his interest in me and suggested we start a relationship. I was not looking for a relationship and preferred us to remain friends and see how things would turn out. Leonard continued to persist as the weeks went by, but I had reservations; he was my boss, and everything was moving so fast. However, I slowly grew fond of Leonard; I admired his positive characteristics, kindness, friendliness, work ethic, ambitions, courage, and faith in God. He was often bold enough to speak to others about God, pray for them, and encourage others to seek a personal relationship with God. He also worked hard and sacrificed a lot for his boss even though he wasn't treated well.

Our bond grew closer, and our conversations became intimate; therefore, I considered the possibility of an official relationship. However, in the depths of my heart, I was troubled by some aspects of Leonard's behavior and character. One major concern I had was his attitude towards other women, mainly how he spoke about his exes. However, it seems that I became blinded by love. Maybe I was desperate in my search to be loved. Before long, his behavior towards me began to change, and moments of intimacy soon became a big concern. Whenever I refused his advances or gestures for sex, I was met with verbal abuse and emotional manipulation. "You must be sleeping with another man. Do you think you are the only woman? I love you, but why are you always rejecting me?" His accusations and tactics seemed to work, and unfortunately, I remained complacent and sometimes coerced. This was no longer a loving relationship but one riddled with abuse.

My concerns became more paramount when we spent more time together. Whenever I talked to Leonard about his behavior, he always assured me how much he loved me, leading me to ignore my concerns. Then, just a few weeks later, I discovered I was pregnant. Leonard was the first person I told. I was in a state of panic. How would my family react? Leonard, however, remained calm and explained that he understood how things may become difficult for me at home. He comforted me and reassured me that he would be there for me and our unborn child. I was thankful for his encouragement and felt comforted and optimistic that I would not be left alone to face the challenges ahead.

In the days that followed, I had some difficult and sleepless nights trying to figure out how best to approach my family about my pregnancy. One evening, I gained enough courage to approach and tell my mother. She reacted with great shock, disappointment, and concern about what was going to happen with my studies. I only had seven months left to graduate. My mother had many questions about the man responsible, as I had not mentioned anything to her about a relationship. However, I withheld my responses because I was unsure of my circumstances and needed time to think.

Challenges began to arise quickly at home, so I went to see Leonard at work to seek his support and comfort. I explained my situation to him; he was very understanding and sympathetic. He consoled me and again promised that he would be there to support me and the baby no matter what. I felt encouraged; however, about a week after our conversation, there was a drastic change in his attitude toward me. He stopped calling and was no longer picking up my calls. I made efforts to see him at the workplace, but I felt unwelcome. Despite my efforts, I could not resolve the situation. Therefore, I had to accept the sad reality that our relationship had broken down. His promise to support me and our baby was no longer valid, and I was unceremoniously thrust into single parenting and forced to fend for myself pre- and post-pregnancy.

I felt so alone. I went to my midwife and doctor's appointments alone, often burdened with stress and worried about the needs of my unborn baby and how I would be able to provide for him. I was still a student, paying international fees and not working with limited finances. It was excruciating facing my predicaments alone, and I felt betrayed by the one person who should have been there for me. However, I was forced to learn a harsh life lesson. Gradually, I accepted my situation and adjusted my thoughts, feelings, and plans. I became determined to fight for my unborn baby, push forward with my final year, and, with anticipation, meet my baby, who had become my ultimate source of strength and motivation.

This was not how I envisioned my life; it was antithetical to the plan I had drafted for my life. I suddenly hit a speed

WAITING IN THE PIT

bump, and my car began to spin out of control, down a direction I was unfamiliar with. Since the birth of David, I have experienced various levels, dimensions, and varieties of pits. I suffered through these encounters, which have left me bewildered, bruised, and broken. With no one to talk with, there were days I spent long hours staring at myself in the bathroom mirror or hiding in my room, crying in silence. Months went by, and at times, I felt I was a total failure in the depths of the pits of pain and hopelessness. I became very desperate.

The enemy had declared war against me and my identity, using the negative, discouraging voices of others, leaving me drained. I became self-critical and unsure of who I was and what I deserved. I felt as though I had to work to earn God's love. Even when I did the right things, I felt undeserving of His love; when I did the wrong things, I felt disqualified and unworthy of His favor. Yet, I continuously cried to God for His comfort and divine help. God used the promise of 1 John 4:18 to kick-start my journey of healing and restoration and renewed my perspective of love.

I heard a powerful sermon in 1 Corinthians 13, verses 3-9, which talks about the characteristics of love. The preacher re-read the verses and substituted the word love with God. For example, instead of "love is kind," he read, "*God is kind.*" This was profound, and though I can't remember all the details, I know it was the word of encouragement I needed.

The Holy Spirit began to breathe life into my crushed soul as even then, I was still in the pit of abuse and enduring its exhausting pain. As time went by, God continued to imprint His words and truth into my heart, and as such, when He led me to the promise of 1 John 4:18, I embraced it with my whole being. There are times I still struggle with feeling worthy of love, but it is no longer about God, only people. I can certainly testify that God has shown me all these characteristics throughout my life, even in the moments when I was in sin.

As I continue to wait for the blessing of marriage, I am no longer in a rush to choose someone for myself. I am glad I'm growing more patient and trusting God to guide me to the man He has chosen for me. God is still the best matchmaker. As He did with Adam and Eve, God will choose the best man to be a blessing to me and my sons and for us to be a blessing to him, too.

Moving forward, I am no longer defined by the pain I have endured. I am no longer a victim but an OVERCOMER because I have found rest in God's perfect love. I am deeply convinced and thankful for the assurance that God loves me more than any man or friend possibly can. I have long surrendered my draft plan into His care, knowing that He has a plan to prosper and give me a good end (Jeremiah 29:11).

Prayer: Father God, thank You for Your tremendous love and for restoring my true identity as your daughter. I am exceedingly grateful for Your favor and the endless blessings You have given my sons. Father God, I pray for Your daughters and sons across the world. Please restore them and draw them closer to You. I pray that they will also find rest in You during their life challenges. I also pray that we will soon be reunited with You and enjoy the ENTERNAL REST in Your presence, as well as the new earth and heaven. Amen.

Meet Maria Urassa

Maria is a native of the beautiful African country of Tanzania. She resides in the UK, a country she has grown to love and now considers a second home. She is a devoted mother of three lovely boys, David, Josiah, and Solomon, who are a precious gift from God.

Maria's self-discovery journey, guided by God, has led her to a profound realization of her identity as a child of God. She believes in the strength of unity and the power of encouragement. Her motto, 'Together we are stronger, divided we fall," reflects her commitment to fostering a supportive community.

Maria's love for sharing poems and inspirational videos is a reflection of her deep faith and the goodness of God she experiences. Her content is a source of hope and inspiration for many. She is also thankful for her newfound passion for hosting and looks forward to connecting with her audience. You can reach her at: email: mariaurassa@yahoo.co.uk

Instagram: *secy_ria*

CHAPTER 21

"It is Done"

66

*Trust in the Lord with all your heart and lean not on your own understanding. In all your ways acknowledge Him and He'll direct your path (**Proverbs 3:5-6**)*

99

Born into a Christian home, Balita learned to pray from an early age. She saw those around her praying, but like many Christian practices, she didn't truly understand their significance until God heard her little heart.

Balita was a cheerful, soft-spirited little girl filled with so many dreams and aspirations. Born on the tiny tropical island of Jamaica, she was the third child of four. Her father was a pastor well-known by many on the island and internationally. He was born in the UK but moved to Jamaica with his family as a youth, where he met Balita's mother, and the rest is history.

Balita enjoyed sports, singing, dancing, and anything that made her smile. She was such a bubbly, fun little girl who lit up the room with her enchanting presence. When she smiled, it was like the sun beaming through a dark room. Balita hated to see others upset, bullied, or abused. She wanted everyone to be happy and would come to the defense of those in distress. If Balita was around, you were sure to feel loved and safe.

If her charismatic character wasn't enough, her light brown skin, pink lips, freckled face, and red hair were sure to draw the attention of others. She was also exceptionally creative and skilled in many areas. She excelled in running, gymnastics, karate, home craft, and more. Although impressively gifted, she also liked to see others win. She would always encourage her friends to join her in developing themselves.

One early summer morning, she sat in her grandmother's home and reminisced on the stories shared by members of the Seventh Day Adventist church she'd attended on the south side of the island. They had shared their testimonies of the many encounters they'd had with Jesus. Though she was born into the faith, she hadn't yet experienced any striking miracles like those shared by the members. As she sat pondering about all the testimonies she heard over the years, she found herself longing to experience Christ personally and tangibly as they did.

She sat in the empty room observing her reflection on the polished red floors that she and her siblings had often knelt and toiled to polish most Fridays using red dye and a pair of dried coconuts. She thought, "Well, they did say to ask, and it shall be given, seek, and you will find." She remembered the preacher saying, "Suffer the little children to come unto me, for of such is the Kingdom of Heaven." She learned that those were words of Jesus giving the disciples a good "telling off" for trying to stop children from coming close to Him as He preached. She felt sure that her six years of age qualified her to go to Jesus and ask anything. She didn't quite understand what it meant to seek, but she had an idea that it may have meant to read the Bible, which was all she kept hearing. "Read your Bible and pray every day." The Sabbath school teachers and AY (Adventist Youth) leaders even had the children reciting it in song:

> *"Read your Bible, pray every day, and you'll grow, grow, grow. Neglect your Bible, forget to pray, and you'll shrink, shrink, shrink."*

Balita began to talk to God. She prayed:

> *"Dear Father in Heaven,*

I know I am just a little girl. If you are as real as they say, can you please take some time to talk to me? I want to hear your voice so I can know you like the people in the church. Brother Clarke said you can stop gun from firing when bad man try to pull the trigger. He said you did that after he called out to you and that you saved Sister Dawkins' house from destroying in a hurricane when everybody else who didn't go to church house got mashed up. God, I want to know you like them. So, I won't be afraid of anyone or anything, not even Daddy.

God, will you make me know what you sound like so I will know when it is You talking? And God, I'd love to be like Mama and help many people. I would like to get married and have children, and if You know me, then You know that I love to dance but mummy them don't love dancing. Every time I hear the music and people on the street, I want to join them. They always have so much fun. Can You please let me get to see what it's like? I won't stay there if it's not good for me, but I just want to know what it's like. I see no one knows when You will come back, but please don't come before I get to experience out there. I promise I'll be good and will tell everyone about You if You just do this for me, please?

And Lord, I really want to be an actress or a singer, but Mummy and Daddy say it can't put food on the table. But I really want this. But if this upsets you, too, I can

*just be like Mama and help lots of people. A nurse will
do. Okay, Lord, I have to go now. My friends are here.
Thank You, Jesus, Amen."*

Balita got up with a big smile on her face as though a great
wish had come true. She ran out to the street and greeted
her cousins and friends. Every day, she waited expectantly
for God to show up and speak to her as she had requested.

Day after day, she met each morning with a new smile. She
enjoyed the company of her only brother. She played video
games, football, and wrestling and climbed trees with him.
She would be there wherever he was because her brother was
her companion.

During communion service, Balita usually watched those
who took part, wondering what the bread tasted like. Only
baptized Christians were allowed to partake in this
ceremony. One day, during a week of prayer at her school,
she watched her peers, and two older siblings scribble their
names on the baptism candidate's list. She thought this was
a golden opportunity to discover what the bread tasted like.
So, she added her name to the list. All she knew was that you
had to say that you believed Jesus died for you and that He
was your reason for choosing to be baptized, and that was it.
She had heard repeatedly that Jesus loved and died for all
humankind. She just didn't know Him personally just yet.

Balita said, "I do," in response to all the baptismal vows read by the pastor, and she was baptized with her siblings. She had no real idea of the solemnity of the covenant she just took. Excitedly, she looked forward to the next communion service; she was now qualified to participate and would finally discover the bread's taste.

When the day arrived, she sat in the pews and waited with her older siblings to receive the communion bread and wine. After breaking the bread, the pastor and elders handed the vessels to the deacons, who served the members pew by pew. When the plate got to her, Balita eagerly picked up a piece, shoved it in her mouth without hesitation, and quickly ate it. As she ate, she thought, "What was the big deal in this? It's not even that good." So much for getting baptized.

Life persisted, and Balita went to church with her family and tried her best to uphold the principles her parents taught her. She maintained a great relationship with her siblings and peers and continued to be a sparkling light everywhere she went until things began to take what appeared to be an awful turn for the worse for her.

Her parents started a business and employed several workers to help around the house and assist in delivering bread across the island. With blind trust and unsuspecting spirits, they sought to develop a congenial relationship with their workers and establish a business that felt like one big happy family. The workers were welcomed in their homes, and few boundaries were established. This left an opening for the enemy, who is always on the prowl to destroy families and tarnish lives. By opening their doors to these strangers they deemed as friends, the family's safety and sacredness began to fray at its edges. Balita, being open and friendly, became a target. The male workers touched and spoke to her inappropriately, even attempting to lure her into things that were not fitting for a child.

Balita had expressed to her mother the discomfort she felt because of the inappropriate conduct of one of the workers toward her. She remembered how embarrassed she felt and how difficult it was to share her emotions. Subsequently, things improved as this "snake" left voluntarily, but the matter was unresolved. She could not tell how her mother felt about the situation because it had not been discussed further. Balita felt safer when he left. Even though the other men displayed inappropriate behavior, they weren't as half as bad as this horrible man. She was also brilliant and learned how to outsmart the workers. She knew how to maneuver her way around without her home without engaging most of them. She learned to protect herself by staying clear of them as best as possible.

Balita was doing well until, to her dismay, her nightmare returned to disturb her. Like a haunting memory, the chief perpetrator was back on the premises as if he had done nothing before. Why was this man in the home again, even after all the concerns she had expressed to her mother?

To her chagrin, the man was installed in the family house and was allowed to share a room with her 10-year-old brother. As close as she was to her brother, she didn't tell him about this man's advances toward her. She now felt robbed of her time with her brother, as she was forced to stay away from his room so she could avoid this man who left her feeling vulnerable and insecure. Every day, she prayed that God would remove him from the home. She tried to contrive a plan with her siblings to eliminate him. Without telling all, she convinced them that he could not be trusted.

Balita realized that if there was ever a time she needed Jesus, it was now. She began praying, asking God to remove this man, but her prayers seemed to worsen things. To Balita, he had a slithering look like a serpent orbiting its prey, waiting for the opportune time to pounce. To everyone, he appeared friendly and innocent. Only he and Balita knew what he was about. "What would he do this time?" she wondered. Every sound of his voice, a touch of his hand, and a glance he cast her way made her cringe.

Weeks passed, and everything seemed normal. Yet, she never felt comfortable. She felt trapped in a pit of anxiety, wondering when next the snake would flick his tongue out and poison her. She only had her prayers to comfort her.

For a while, "the snake" hadn't given her a reason to suspect a pounce. Thus, Belita began to think that maybe God had answered her prayers and changed him. After all, he was a churchgoer. She began to let her guard down and revisited her brother's room, spending time playing, wrestling, and catching up on children's issues. Things got even better when another church member was employed and joined her brother and "the snake" in the room. This new tenant, even though he was short in stature, made her feel safe. He had the most beautiful smile, with the whitest teeth and dimples like hers.

When he arrived, he walked into the room with a guitar in his hand and said, "Hello," then introduced himself as Clarence. He carried a pleasant presence. He would sing and play songs that seemed to wake every corner of the house, making the atmosphere light and merry. His arrival brought back Balia's sparkle. He helped her with her studies and encouraged her to recite poems. He even taught her family songs.

Balita almost forgot the snake's presence until she fetched a toy from her brother's room. Like a true perpetrator, he saw his golden opportunity, as neither Balita's brother nor Mr. Clarence was in sight. He quietly snuck into the room behind Balita and backed her up into a corner. Her parents were away working, as they often did. He took off his belt and threatened to use it if she made a sound.

Could her father's karate lessons be helpful now? If she screamed, maybe her brother would run to her rescue, team up with her, and beat him up. She thought for a moment about running and screaming before immense fear set in and paralyzed her. Before she could fight the paralysis, he wrapped the belt around her neck and threatened to increase the tightness if she did anything to prevent him from continuing his mission. Balita lost hope and froze. All she could do was cry. The pain crushed not just her body but more of her soul. She felt surely there was no God. Her cry was so loud, loud enough to crack every vessel in her body, yet not loud enough for anyone to hear. Not her brother, sister, father, or mother. She felt defenseless, hopeless, and broken like a stream that saw no rain.

That moment seemed to have no ending. Every effort he made tore away at parts of her that were never explored. If she were to survive this ordeal, surely no one would believe anything she'd have to say about this man. He had a good reputation and was deemed "prim and proper" in the eyes of others.

Just as she felt all hope was lost, in walked the heavenly appearance of the musical human being. Clarence stepped in, grabbed hold of Balita's arm, and lifted her to his side as he faced the perpetrator. He then pushed him through the door with one hand. In hot fury, he put him in his place. At that moment, Balita thought of Clarence as the Sampson she'd read about in the Christian storybooks. She was happy he had come to her rescue but traumatized by the few minutes of horror this man had tattooed on her psyche.

For years, this encounter left an imprint on Balita. She felt God had let her down during her turmoil. She wondered why God, who claimed to love her, allowed this terrible thing to happen. She almost lost hope. But God had heard her cry. He had heard her prayer, but her sorrows overwhelmed her that she could not see. She was glad to be free when her "Sampson" stepped in. But in the aftermath, she was filled with many questions and resentment. "Why?" "Why did You turn up so late?" "Why did You allow him to hurt me? Just why?" The outcome was enough to awaken a spark of curiosity that God used to expand her wisdom concerning His true character. God had already answered her prayer; it didn't look or feel like anything she'd expected.

It wasn't until the age of 25, after various life experiences, that Balita finally recognized that God had begun answering her prayer in that moment of turmoil. The little girl's prayers in grandma's home were met with, "It is done." Her requests were granted but fulfilled in stages, according to His will and His timing. It took a surge of events before she recognized that God had answered in that very moment when she'd prayed that prayer in Grandma's room.

The story of Job and Joseph in the Bible enticed an interest in knowing more. They had both gone through severe trauma and were allowed to suffer attacks from the enemy even though God loved them. She began to search the Scriptures with all her heart and found that God allows His children to suffer, but He always has a plan to redeem them all for His glory. Now, she was able to see that God took delight in her will to know. She had found grace in His eyes and became His chosen vessel for His glory.

She realized that God had allowed the perpetrator to only go so far, but not enough to destroy her. Just as with Adam and Eve in the beginning, God had a plan of redemption before they sinned. It was finished before it began. The plan was set. Satan thought he was wiser than God and thought he could win by tempting His creation to disobey and turn against God. But when Jesus' blood was shed, and He gave up the ghost, He said, "It is finished." The battle was already won but wasn't revealed until Jesus rose from the grave. It was then Satan knew that it was over! He had lost, and Jesus had won the victory.

Balita now understood that we may go through some grave experiences, but God has a plan for everything. We may not fully understand how it will pan out, but He plans to give us an expected end: victory! Just as Jesus trusted His Father, Balita knew it would take trust and obedience to God to go through this life, even in times when she didn't understand. As she received this revelation, she was convicted of confessing her errors in doubting and baptizing with the wrong intentions to the Lord. She was now born of the spirit and convicted to be born of water in truth. Balita consecrated herself to the Lord and was baptized in her youth.

Since that moment, her prayer life has strengthened, and she has found a greater appreciation for things of God. What appeared to feel and look like a disappointment was a designed plan of assignment to teach her and many others so that no other, but God would receive the glory.

Even though the snake had slithered his way into her innocence, peace, and happiness, it was God who delivered her in the nick of time and spared her from the total onslaught of this predator.

She realized that her predator, "the snake," much like Satan, "the serpent," and "the dragon," is nothing but a weak usurper preying on the innocent to rob us of our sparkle and our joy. But like Clarence, Jesus, our Savior, and Redeemer, will not allow him to conquer or destroy us. Balita had prayed a sincere prayer. She wanted to know Jesus. She desired deeply to know His voice. Her cries were unheard by those close to her, but God's ears and eyes were open to her cries. God had set in place a plan from the beginning. What was designed to destroy her, God had already imprinted a mark that would only become clear in time. His time.

As Balita waited in her pit of trauma and turmoil and learned, may you wait with expectancy, trusting God to reveal His hand and His heart to you, knowing that one day, the snake that preys on God's innocent children will be crushed once and for all. God is faithful in completing what He started. So, consider it already done and walk in victory!

"When Jesus therefore had received the vinegar, he said, It is finished: and he bowed his head, and gave up the ghost" **(John 19:30).**

Written by: Samantha Howson
Date: 30th April 2024

Meet Samantha Howson

Samantha is simply a pilgrim passing through on a conquest to love and serve the Lord God with all her heart, mind, body, and soul. She's a mother of three God-given seeds and takes the parenting mission as an honorable duty endowed by the Father of Heaven.

Samantha desires to live and share God's goodness through the experiences that God has permitted her to endure. She lives with purpose, in purpose, for the purpose of Jesus Christ, who has saved her lifetime and again. Her life's mission is to continually learn how the Holy Spirit communicates and unwaveringly trust and obey the voice of the Lord in love because "God is love."

Made in the USA
Columbia, SC
05 August 2024